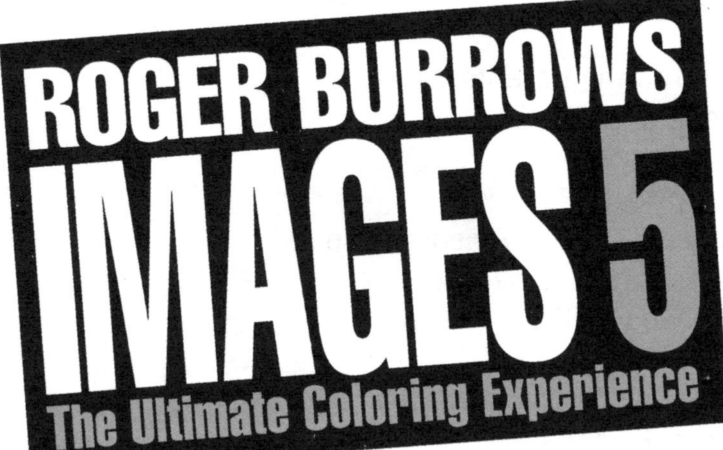

RUNNING PRESS
PHILADELPHIA • LONDON

Dedicated to my parents
Jeanne and Steve

Printed in the United States of America

9 8
Digit on the right indicates the number of this printing

ISBN-13 978-0-7624-1448-2
ISBN-10 0-7624-1448-0

This book may be ordered by mail from the publisher.
Please include $2.50 for postage and handling.
But try your bookstore first!

Running Press Book Publishers
2300 Chestnut Street Suite 200
Philadelphia, PA 19103-4371

Visit us on the web!
www.runningpress.com

INTRODUCTION

In the instant when you are not sure what something is, your visual imagination is released and you begin to see things differently. Shapes, pictures, and patterns come together in unique and different ways—and from this springs creativity!

Images 5 is a new collection of designs to stimulate the imagination. There are 21 new types of design inside that repeat again and again. And on the next few pages, you'll find some notes and suggestions about how to look for images hidden within.

Look at the designs for a while before you start to color them in. One exercise for your imagination is to try and see different things in the same design. For example, look for a shape or picture, then let it disappear from your visual imagination and replace it with something else. Another exercise is to find a shape, or thing, or animal, and then look for it again and again—you'll find it rotated and reflected, as well as the same way up.

Imagination is the ability to see things in new ways, to juggle and change things in your "mind's eye." These designs have been created to help build your imagination and to apply the unique creativity that is within you.

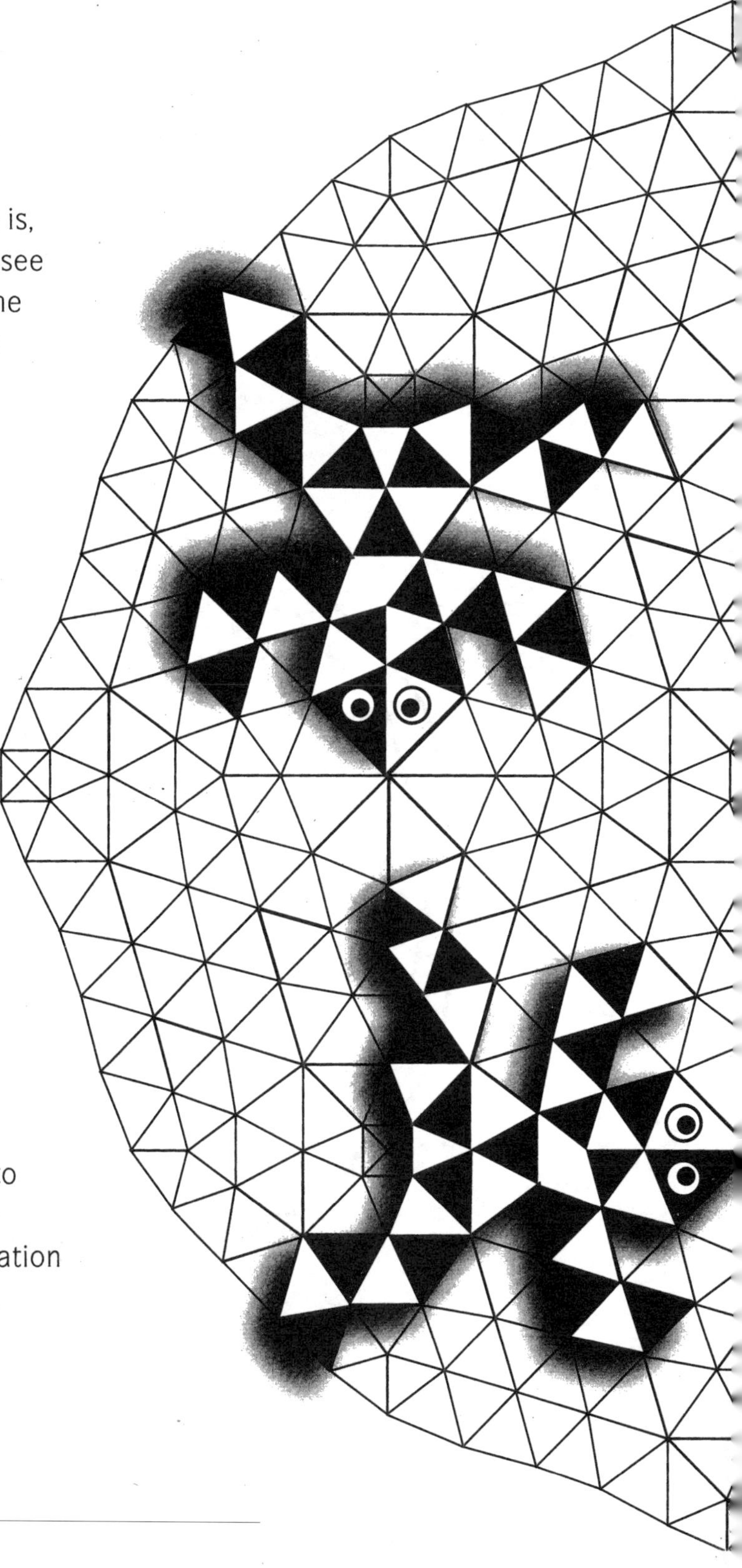

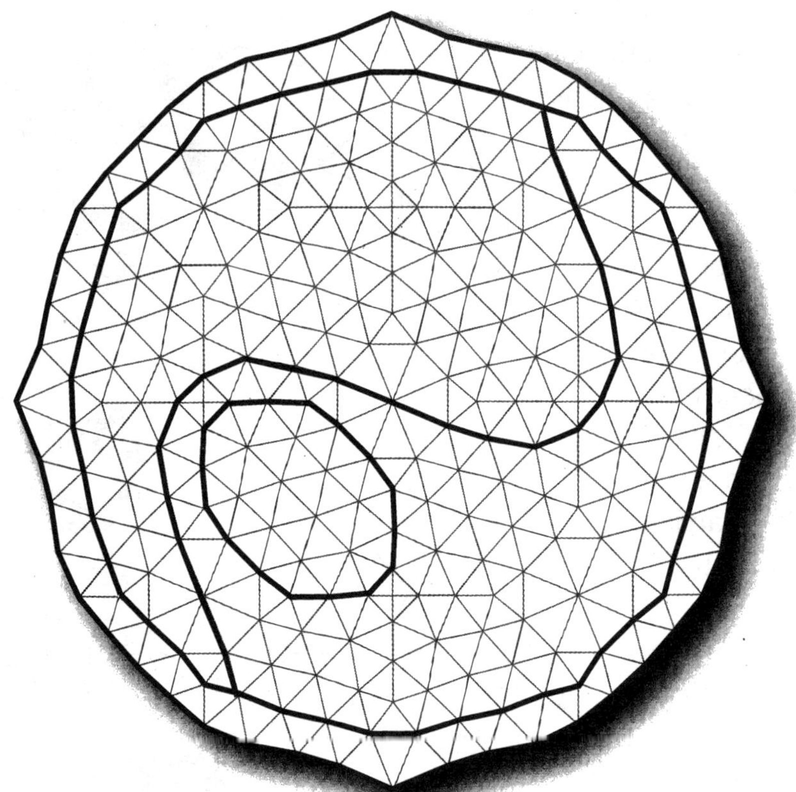

This is just an example of some of the shapes that can be seen in this design to the right. Remember that, whatever shapes or pictures you find, you can find them again and again—the same way up, but also rotated and reflected.

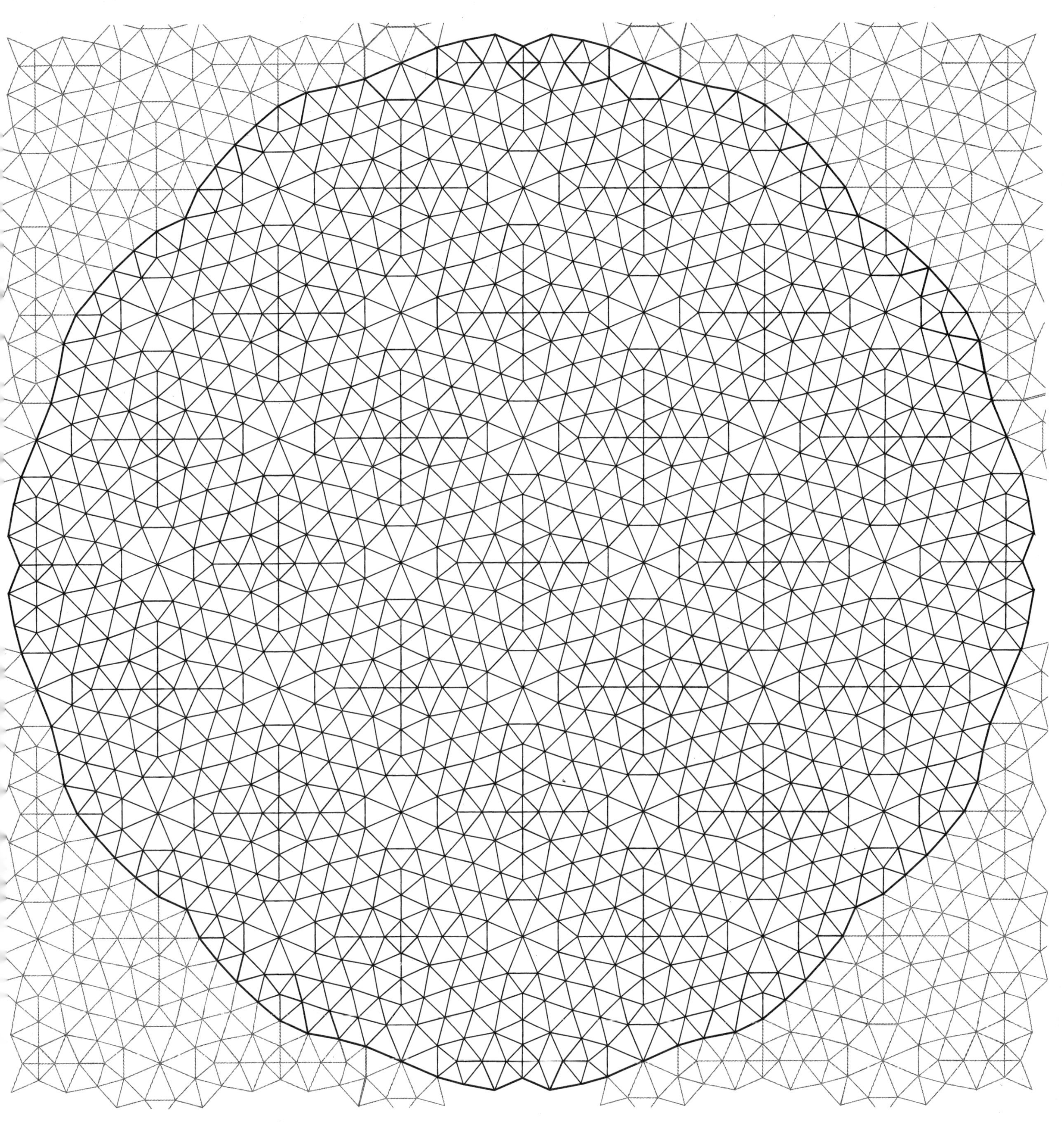

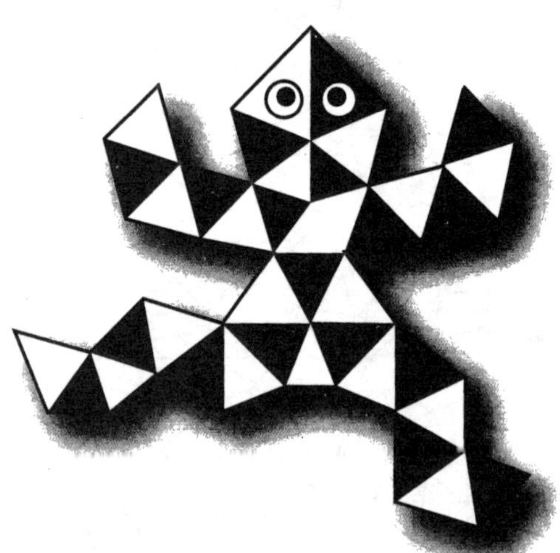

Can you find this little character in the design to the right? Remember that, whatever shapes or pictures you find, you can find them again and again—rotated and reflected.

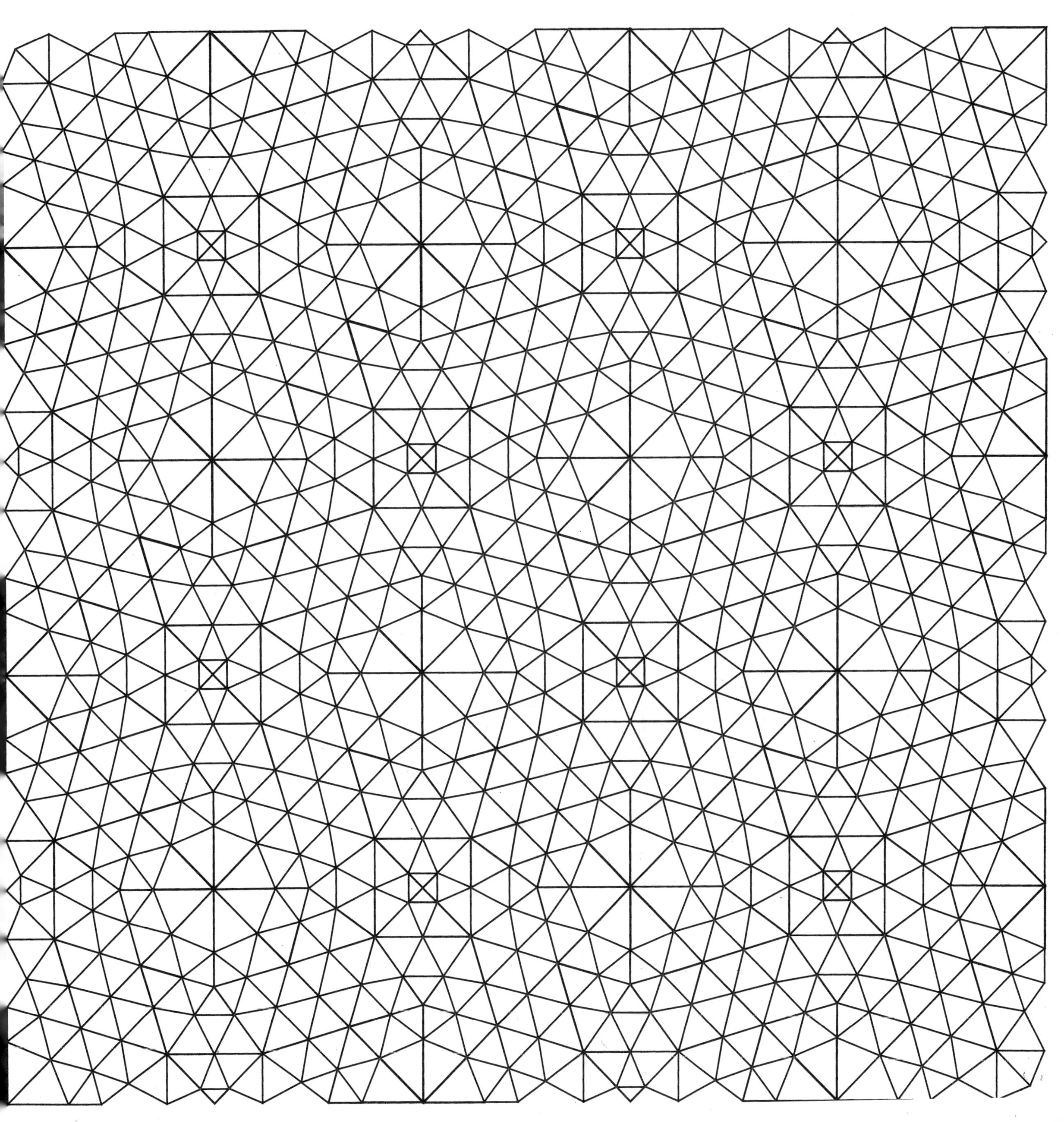

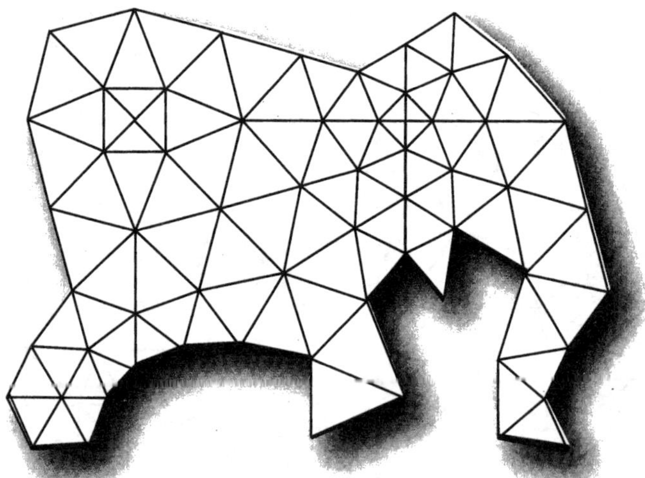

Can you find the elephant in the image to the right?
Look for it forwards, backwards, and upside-down.

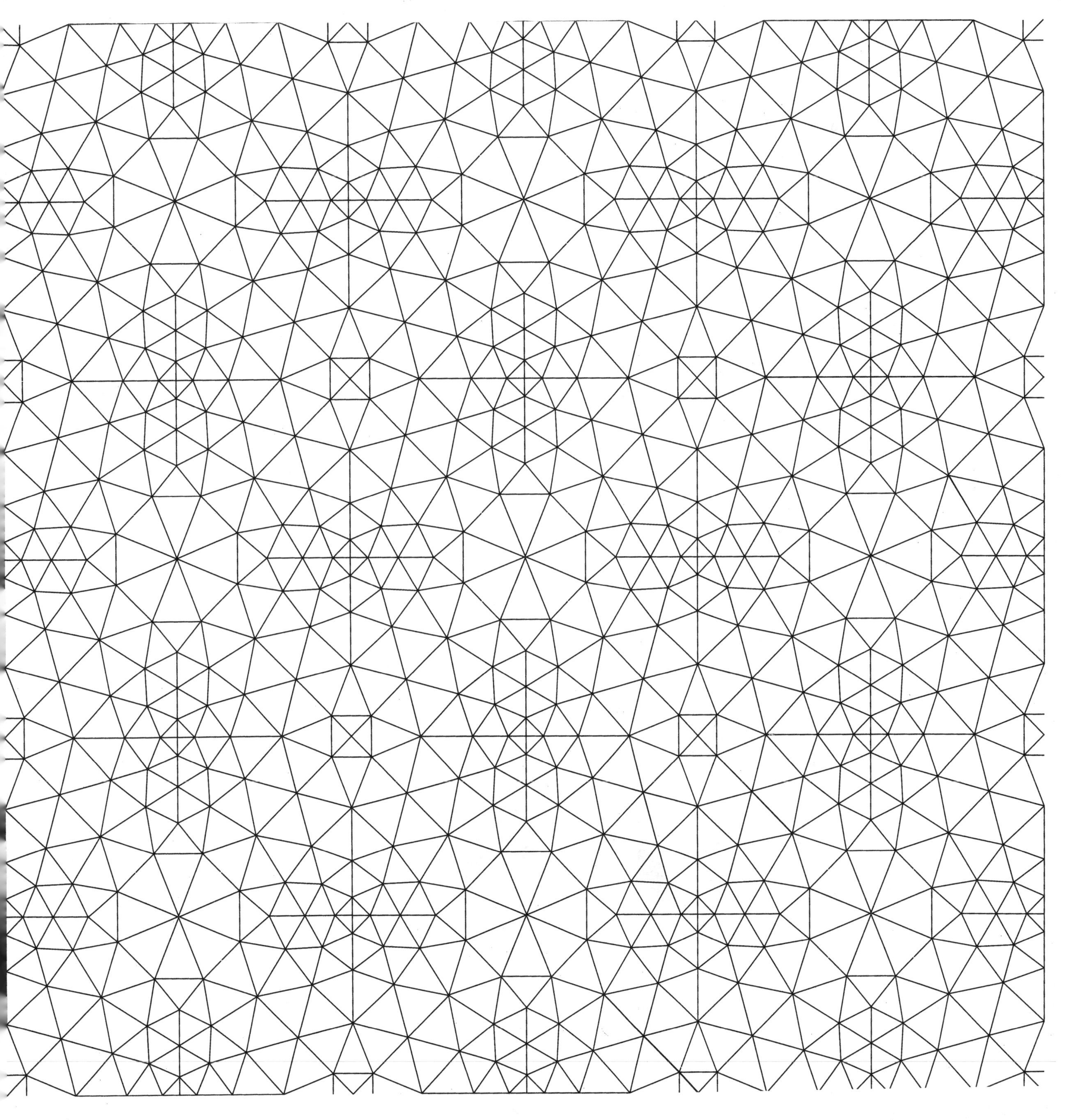

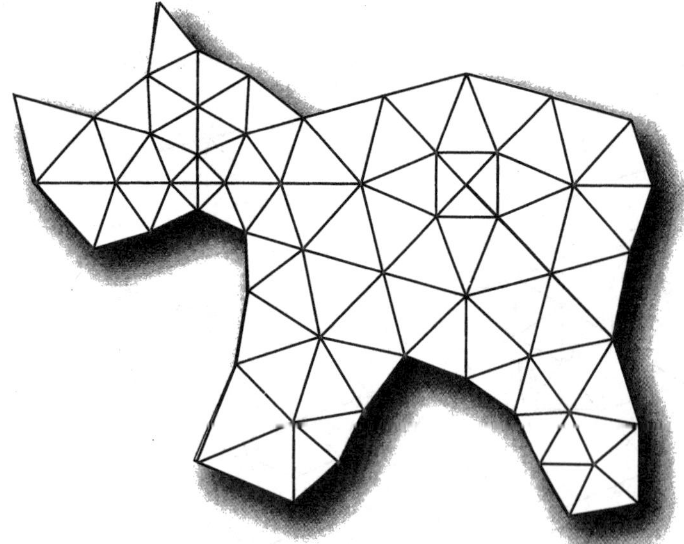

Can you find the rhino in the design to the right?

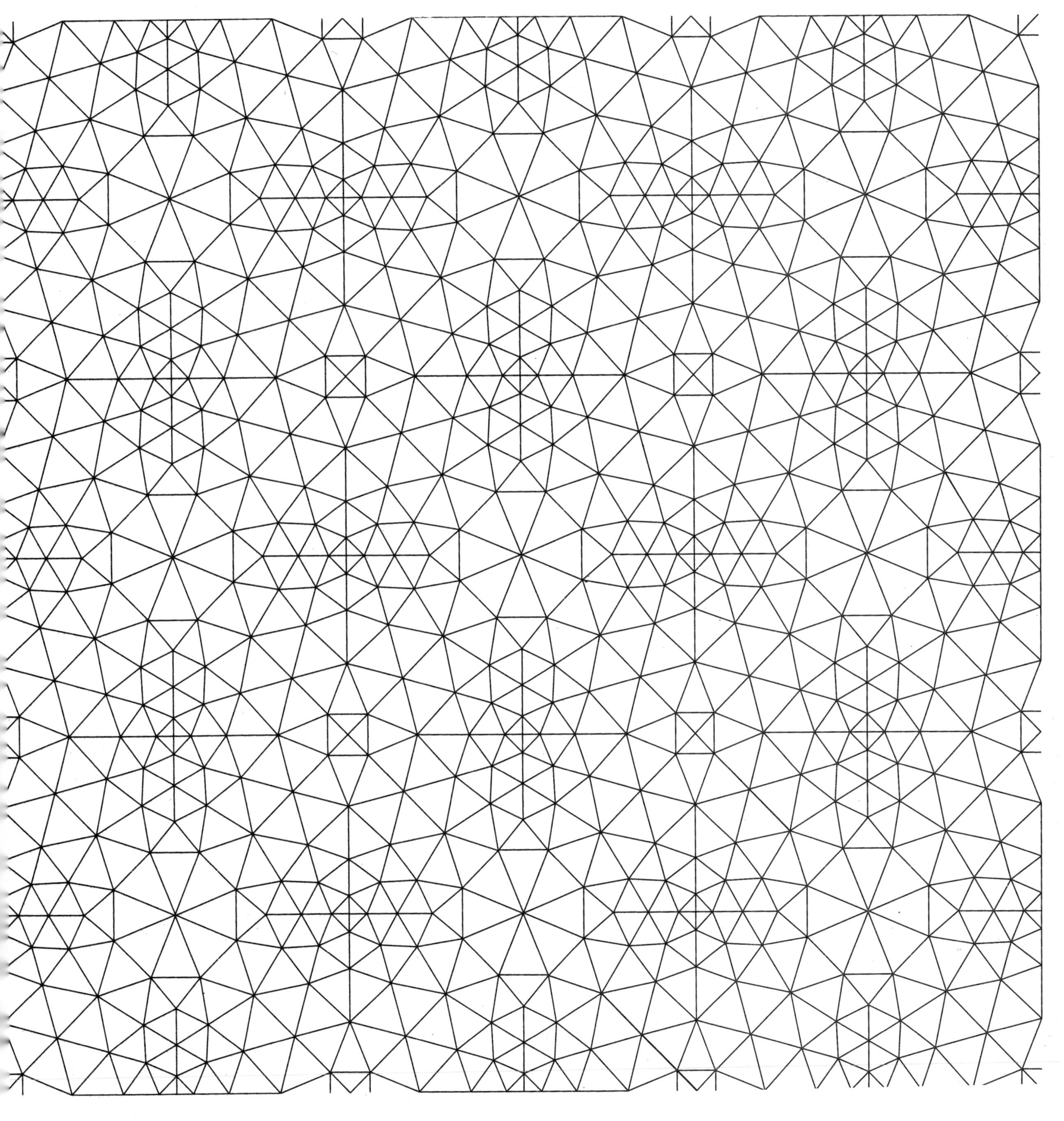

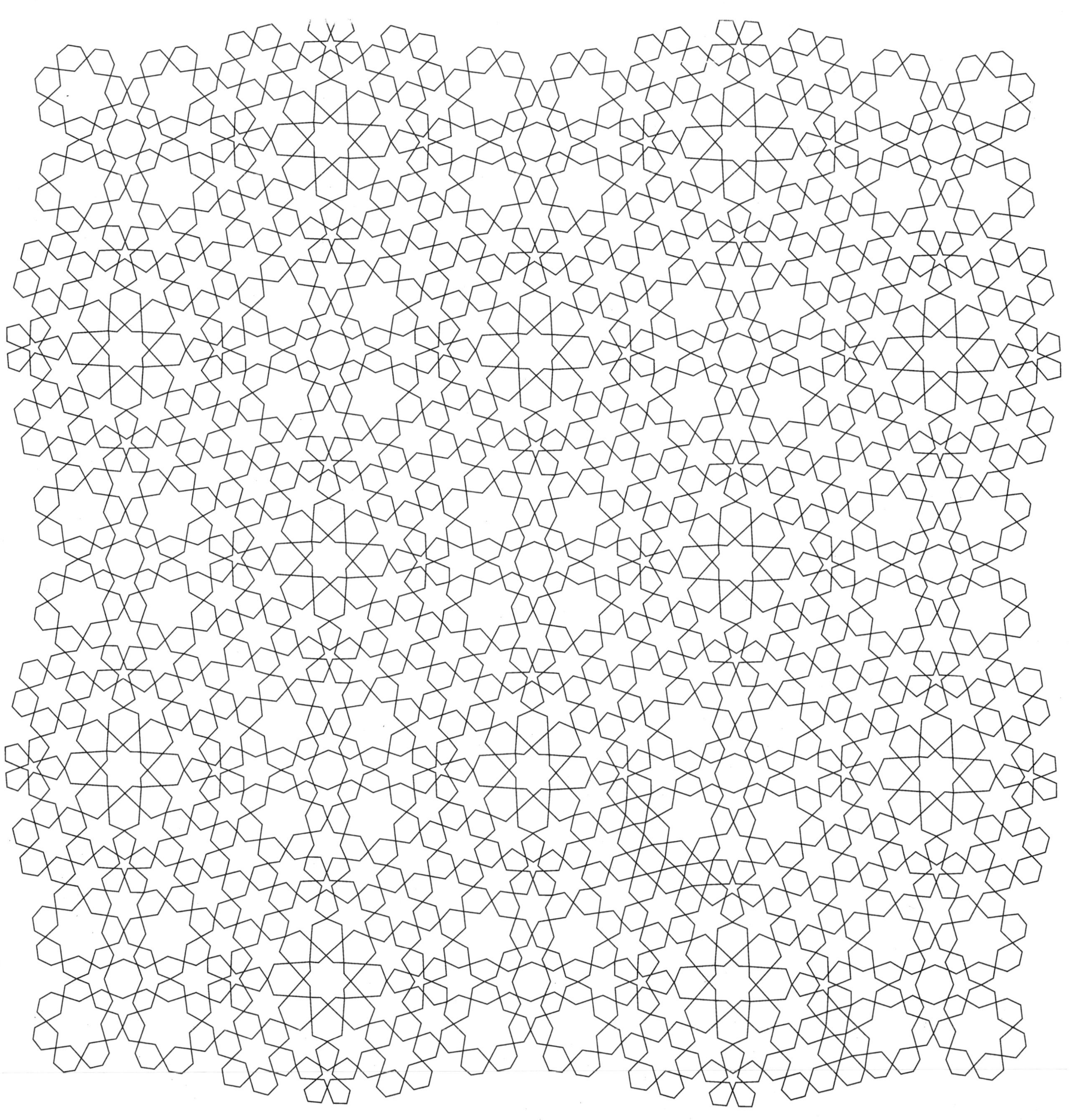

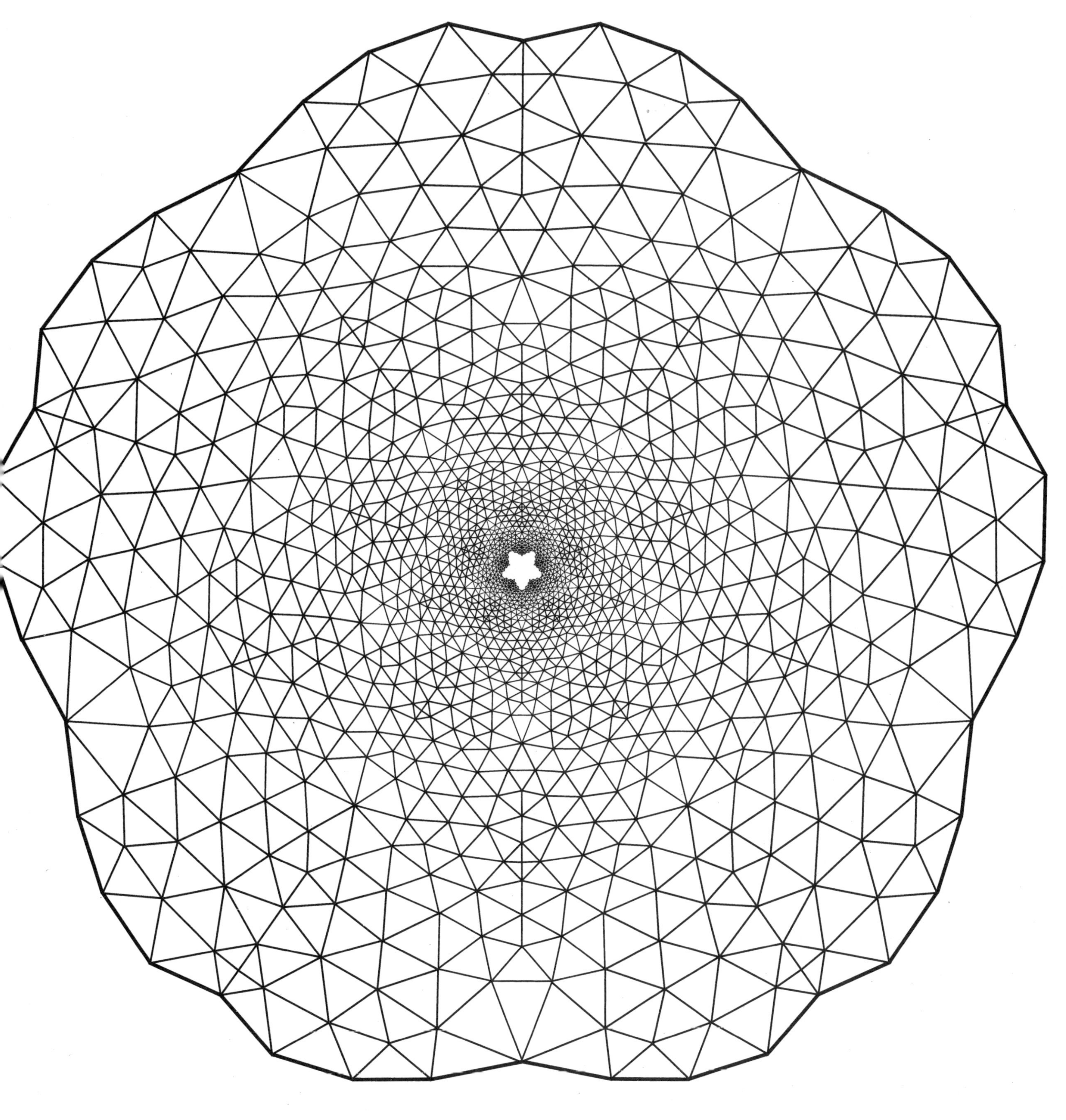

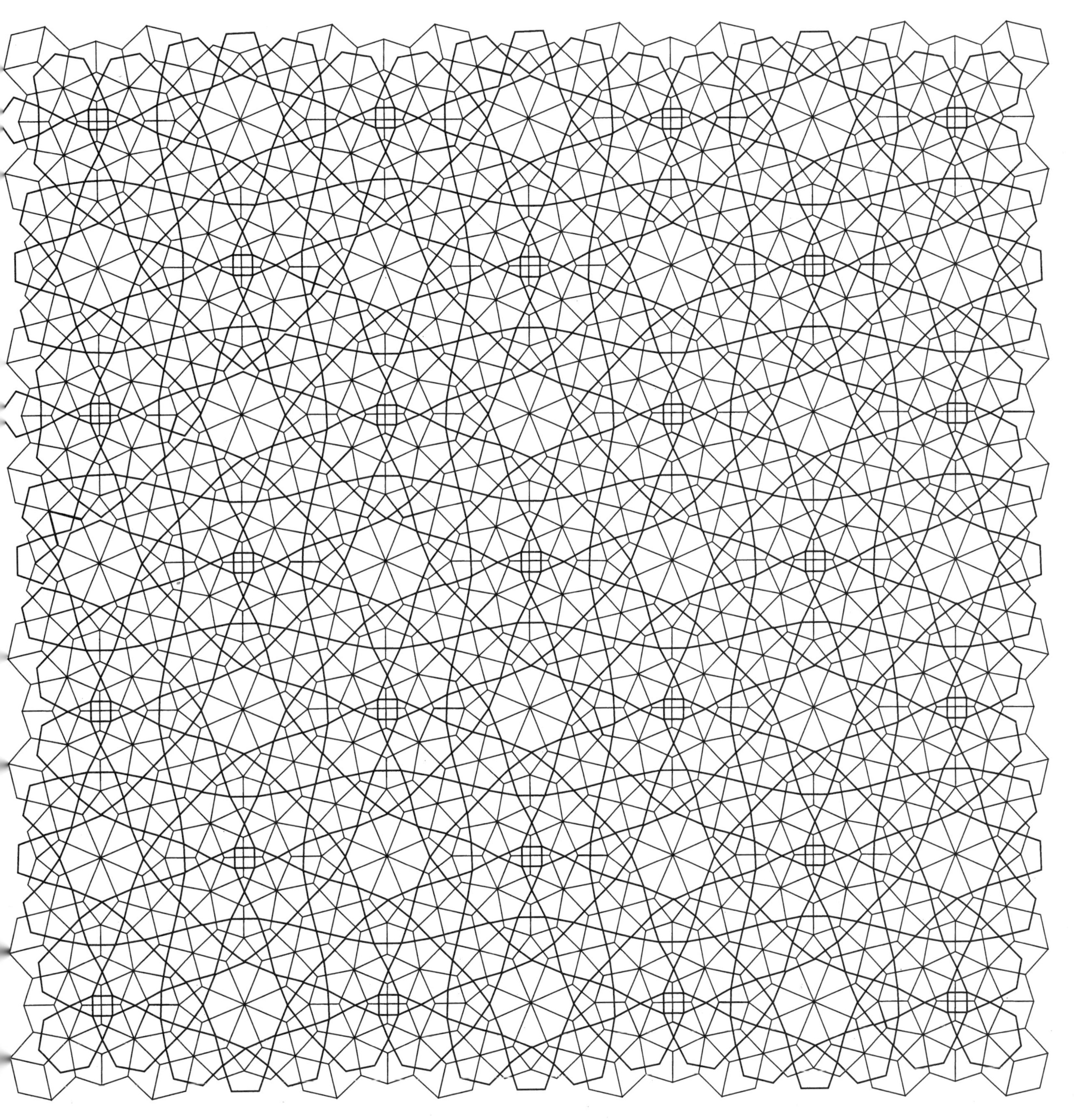

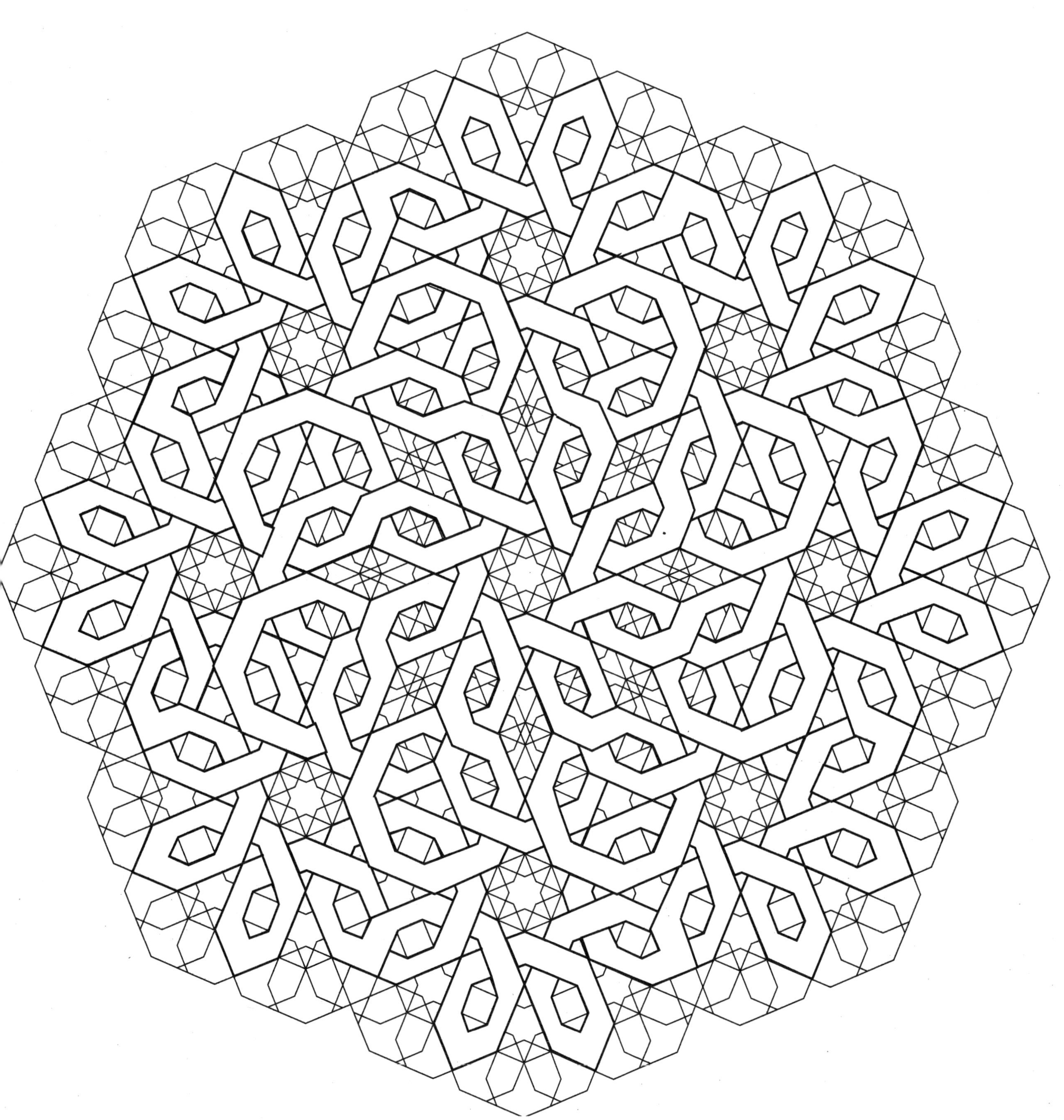

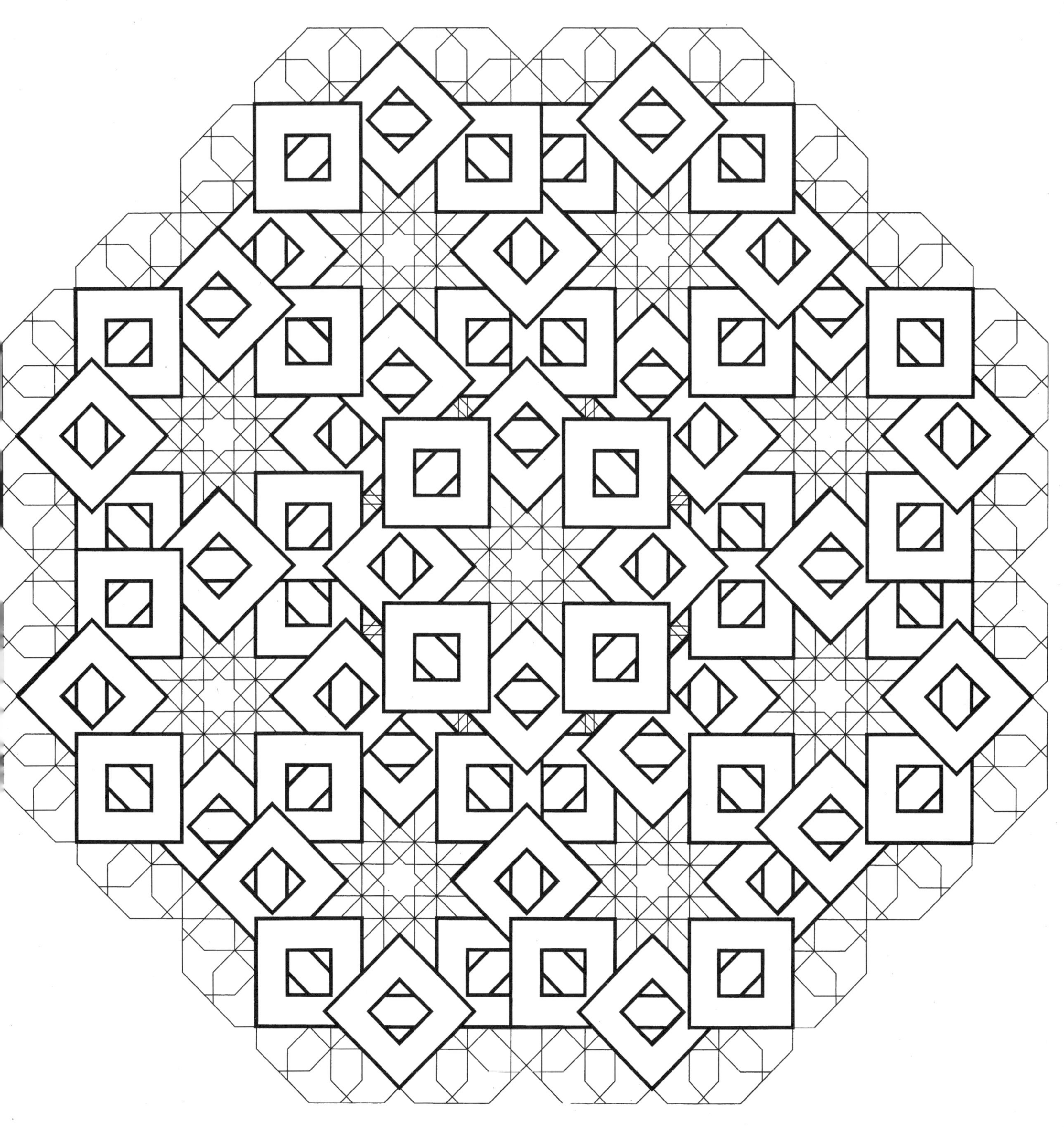

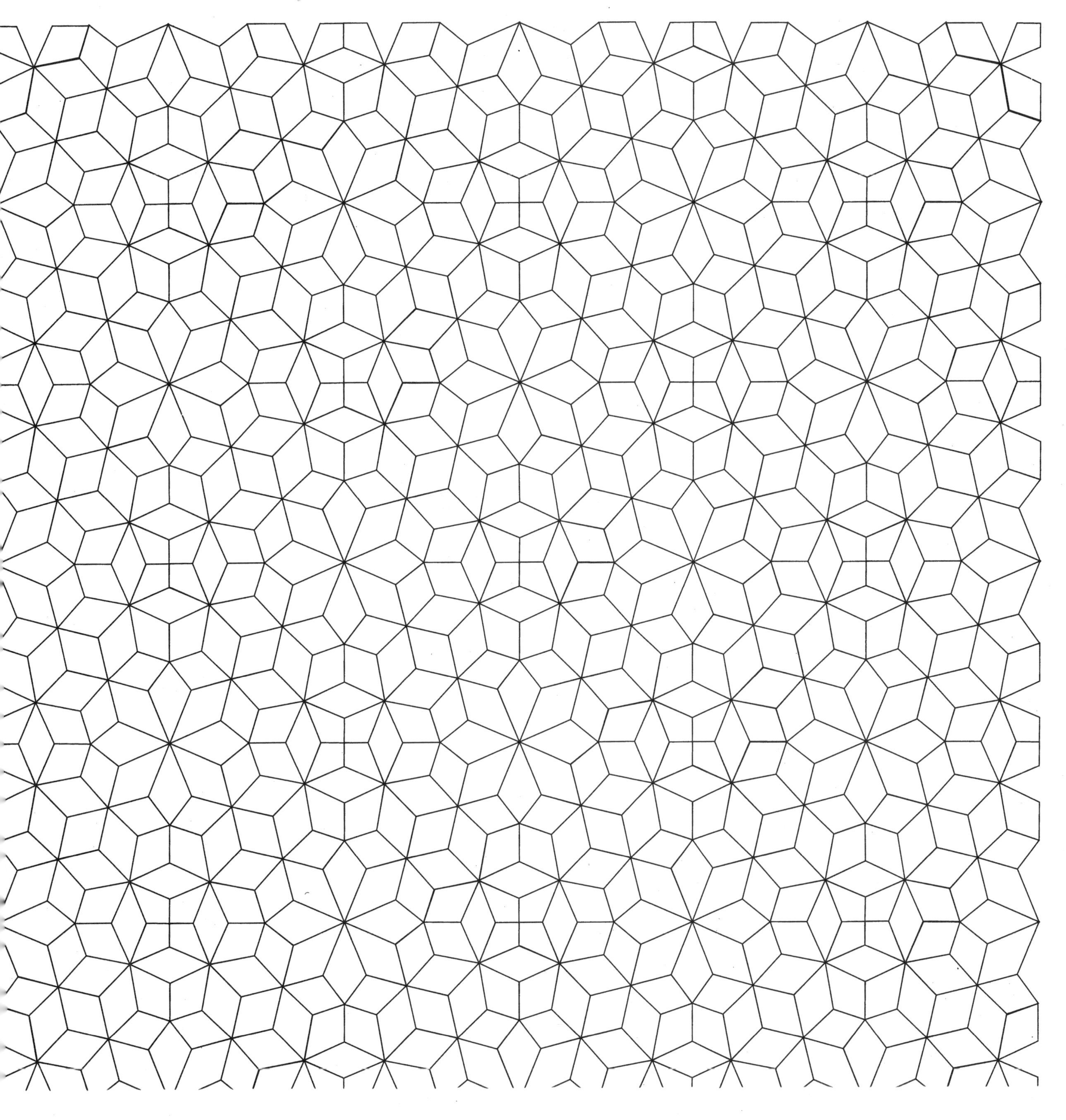

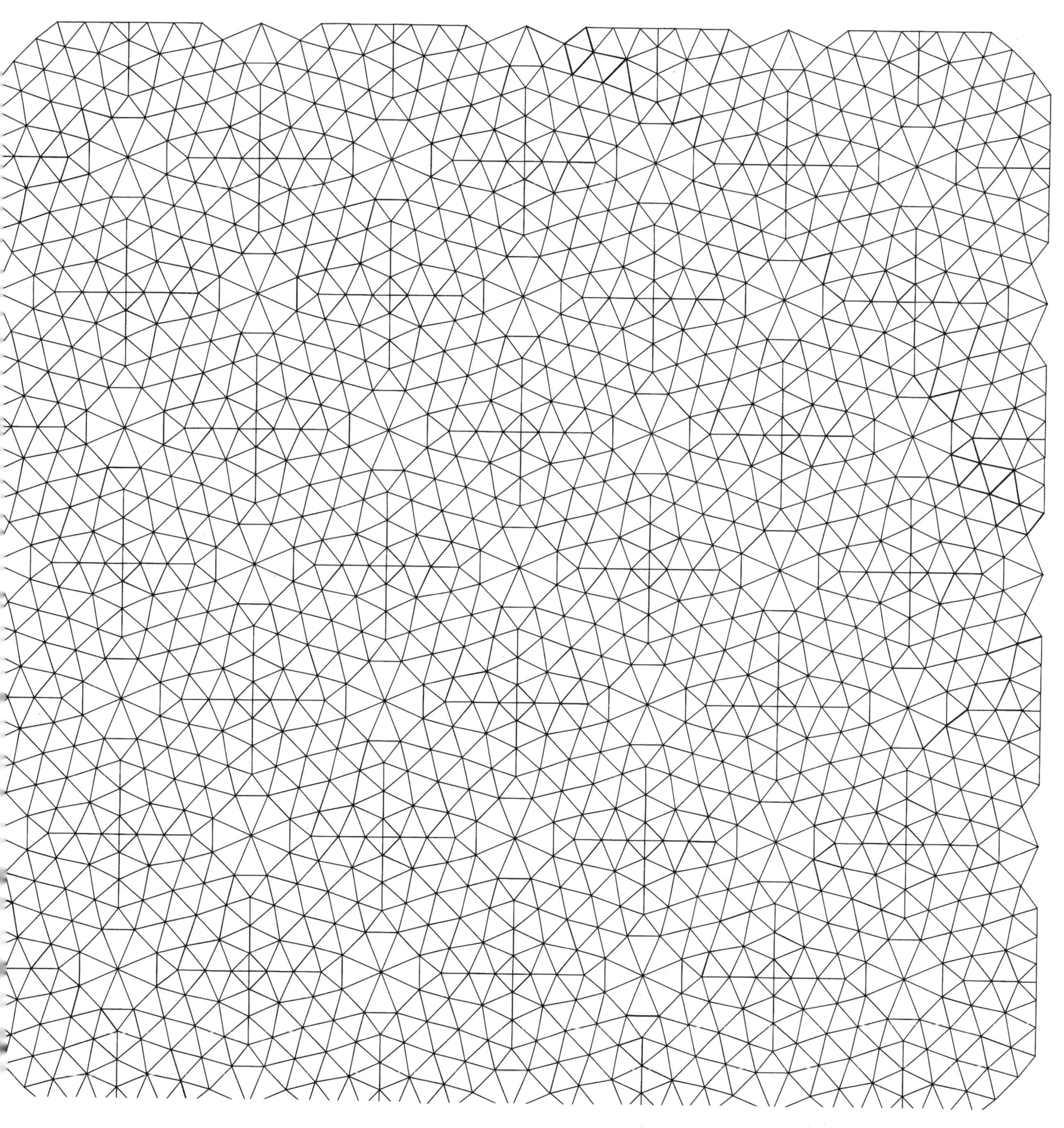

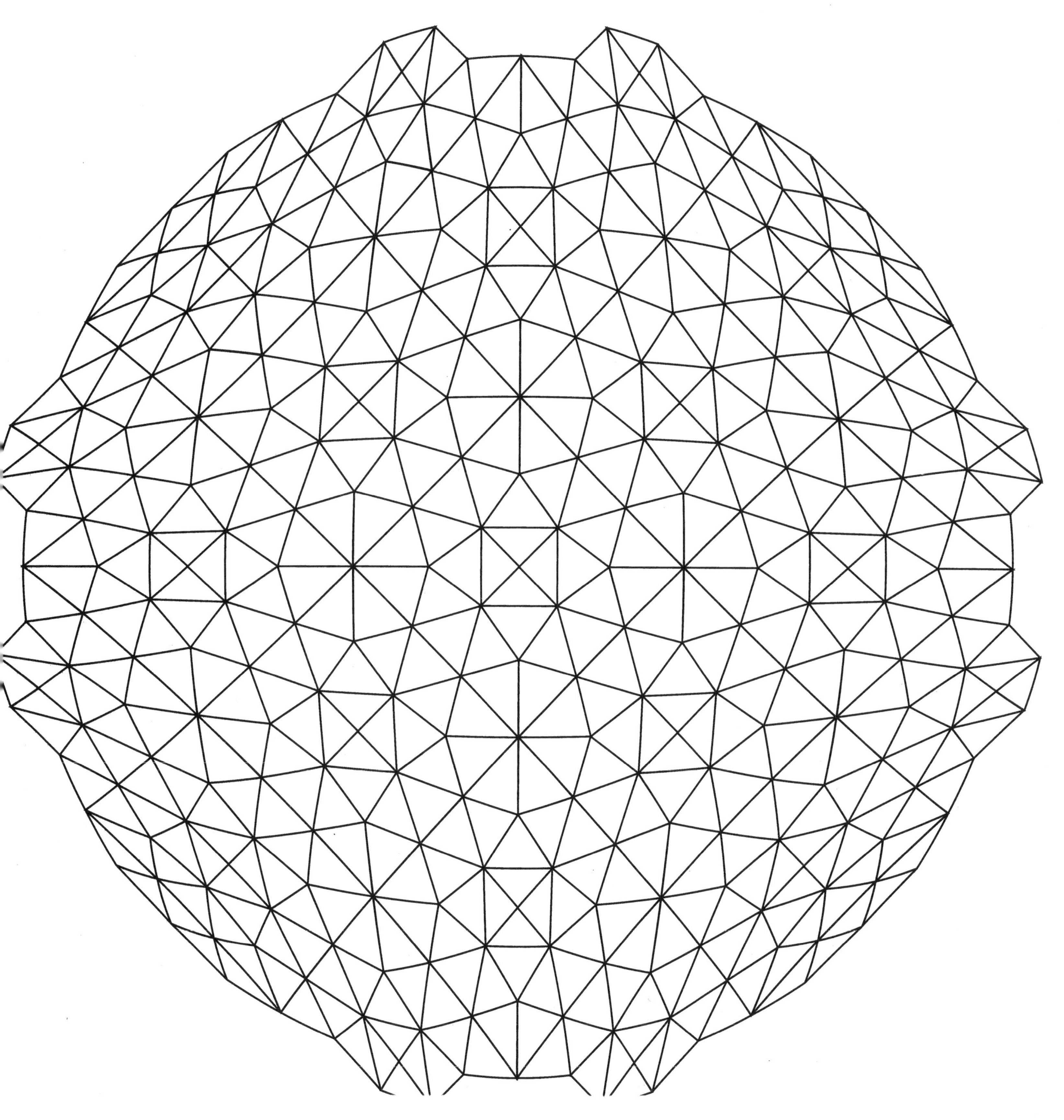

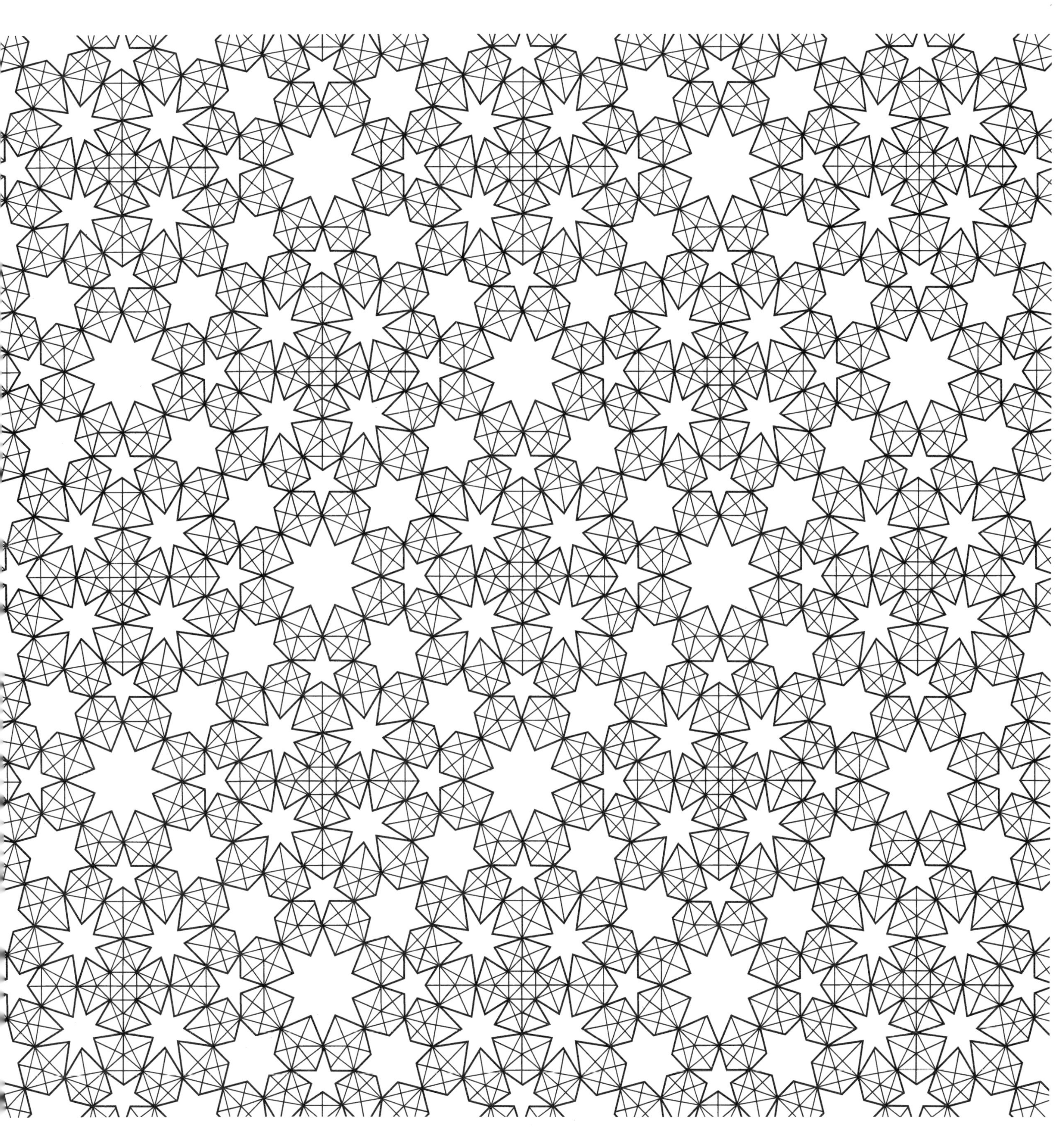

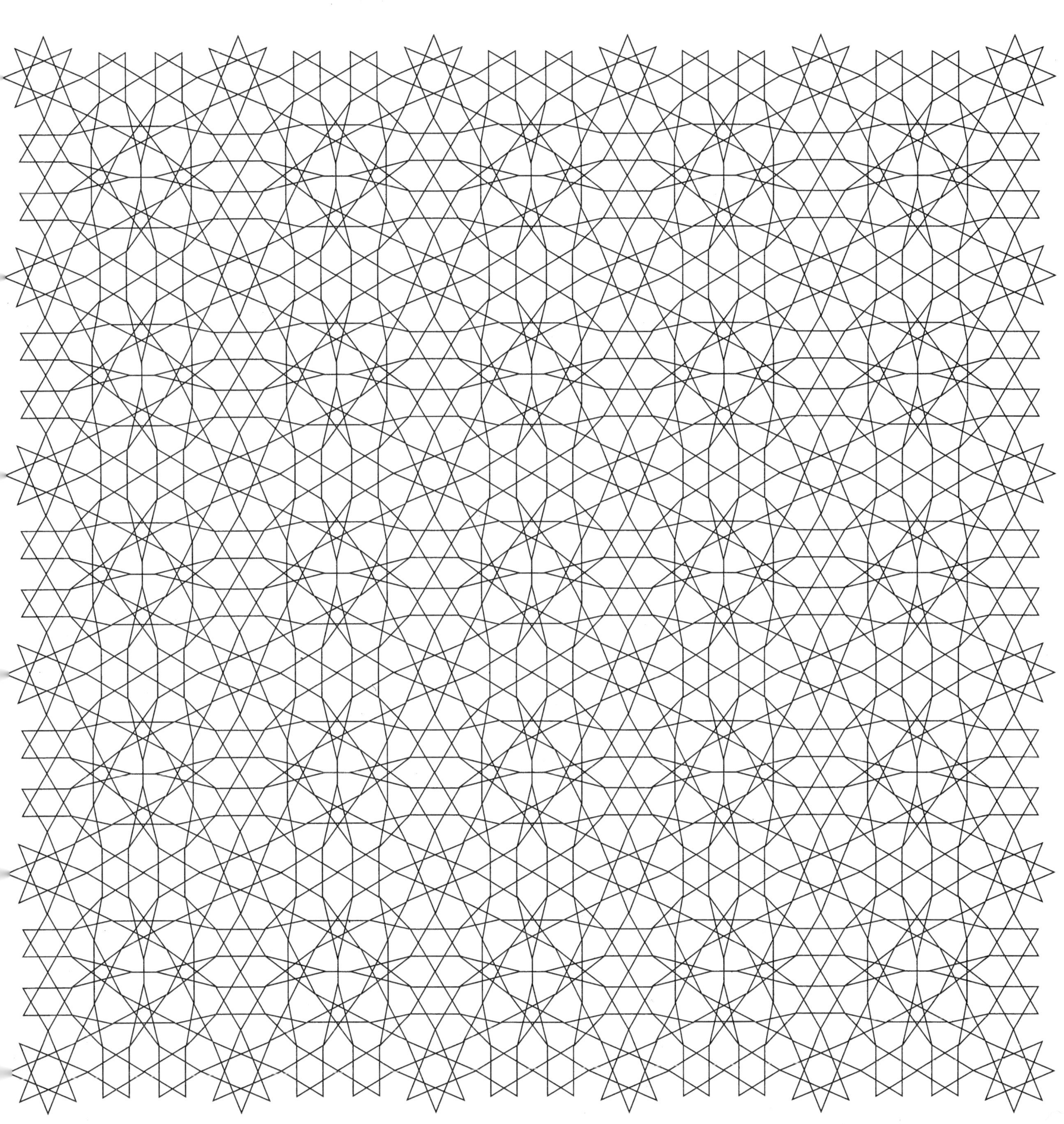

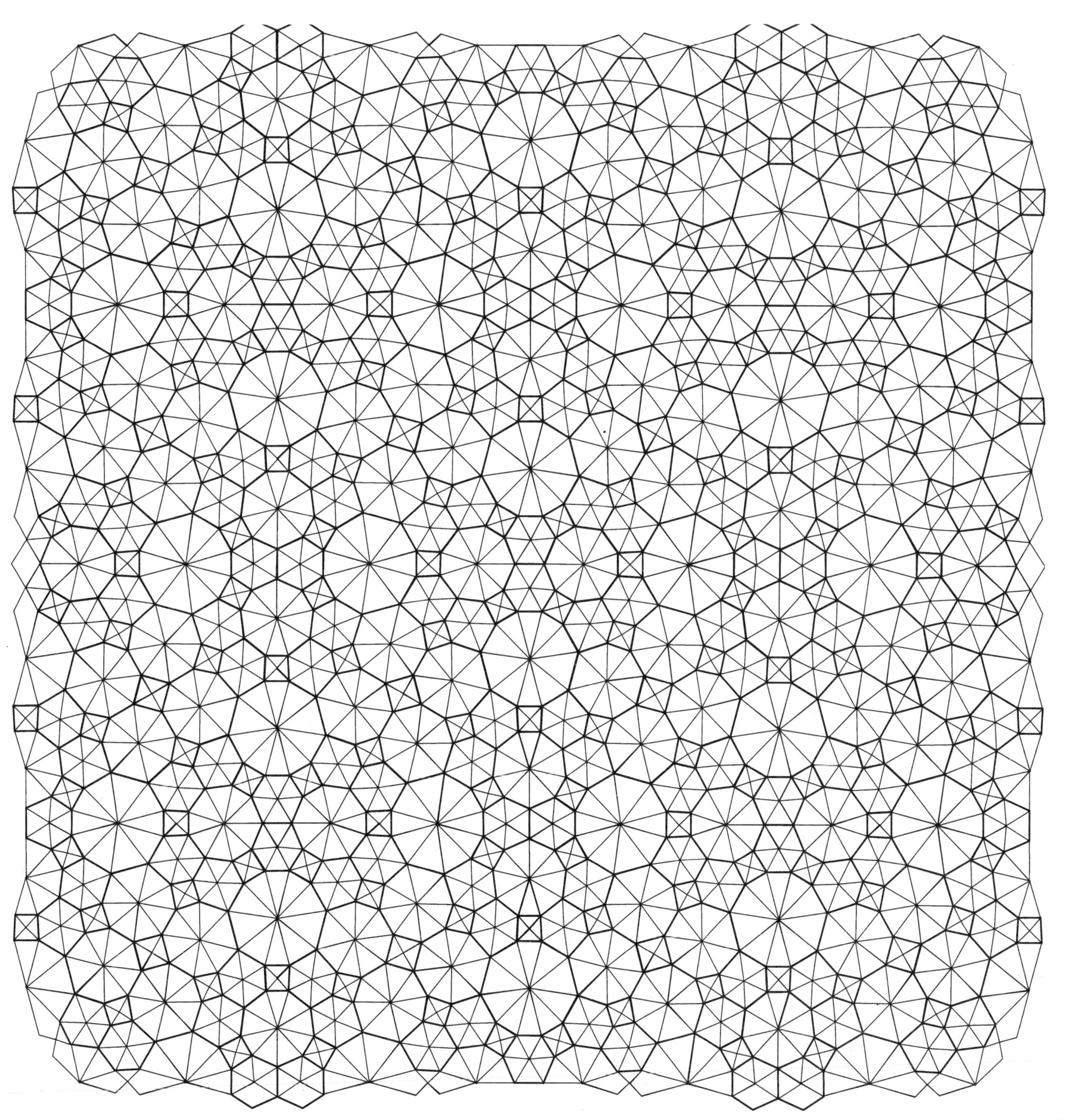

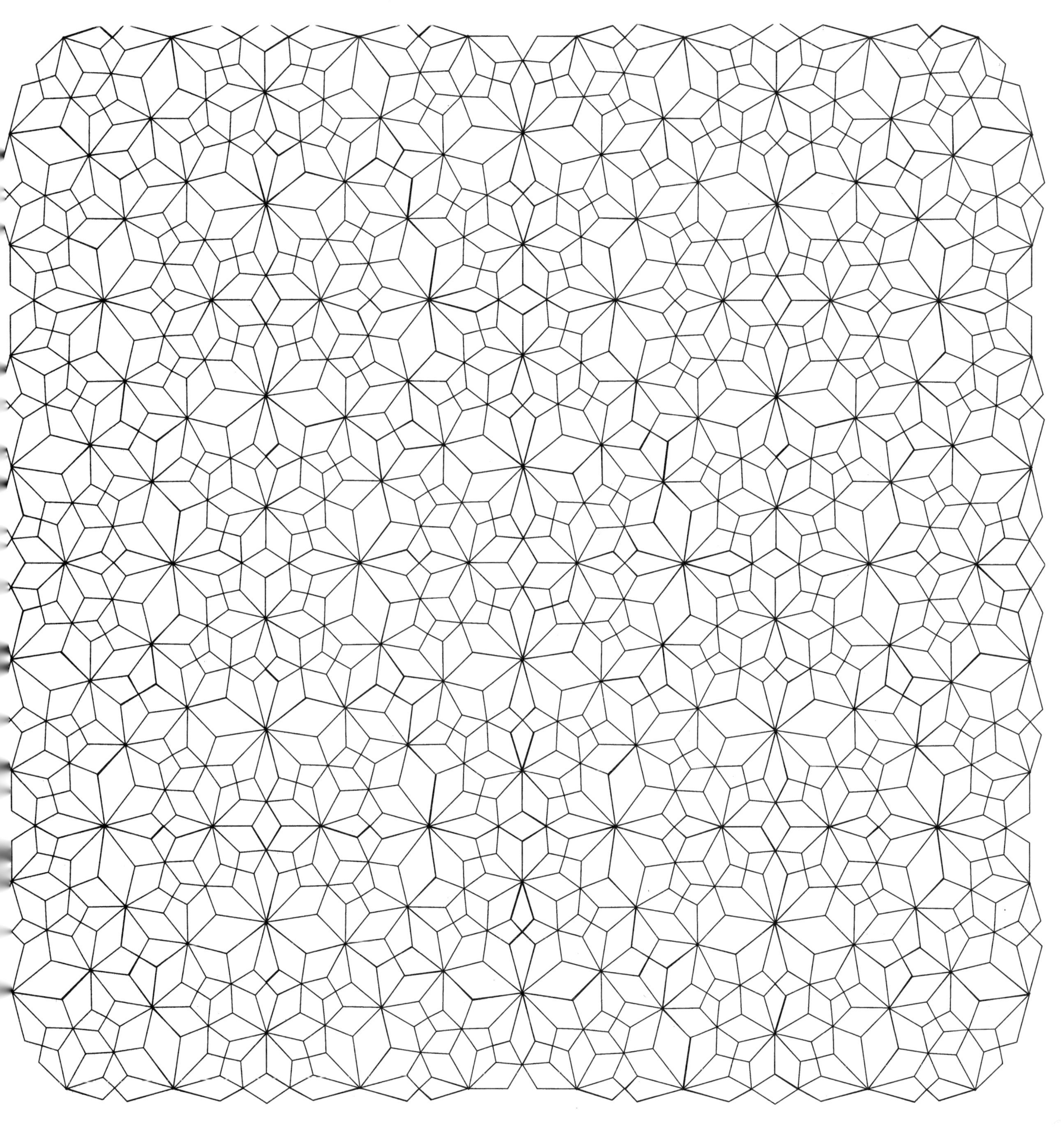

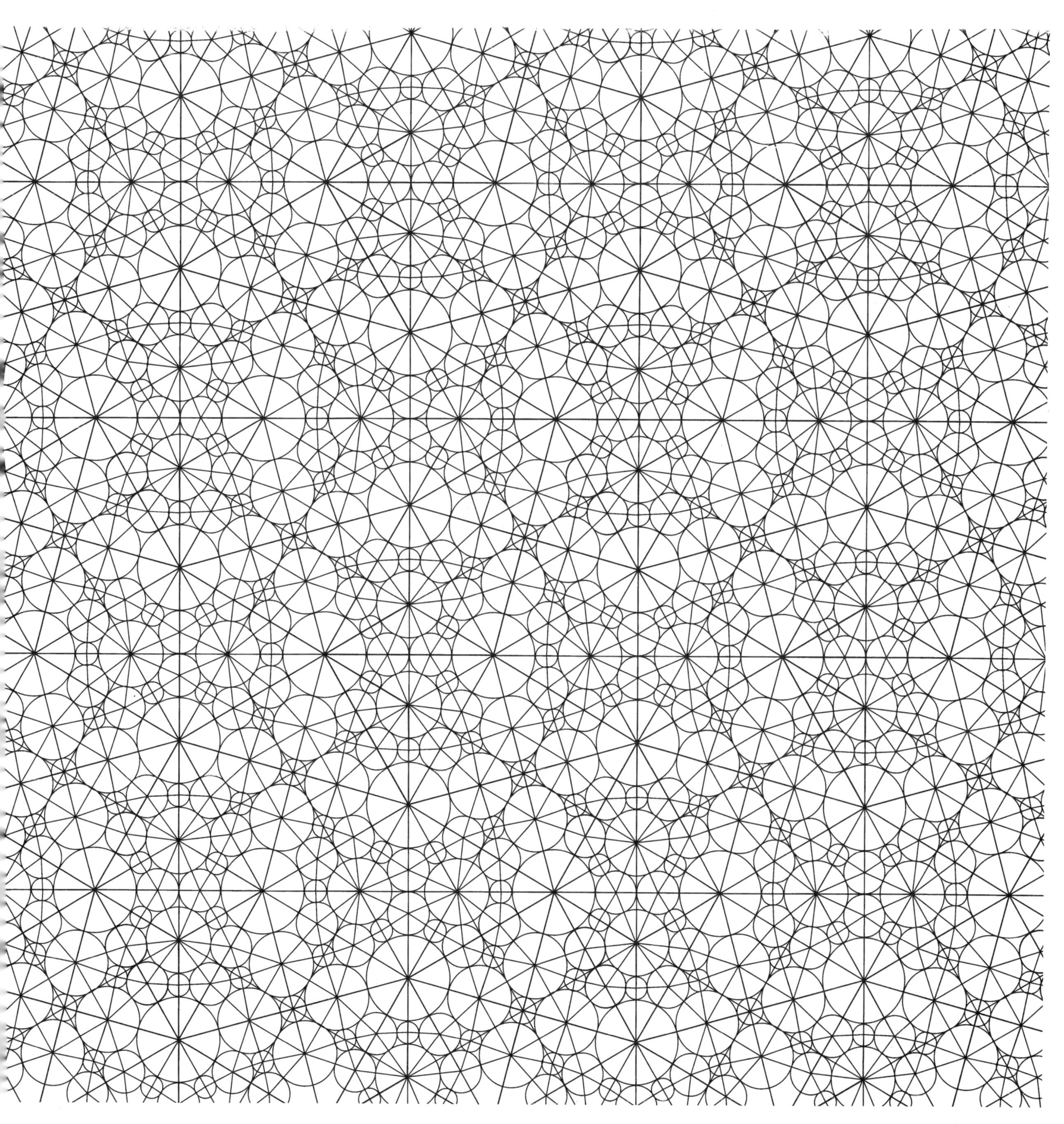

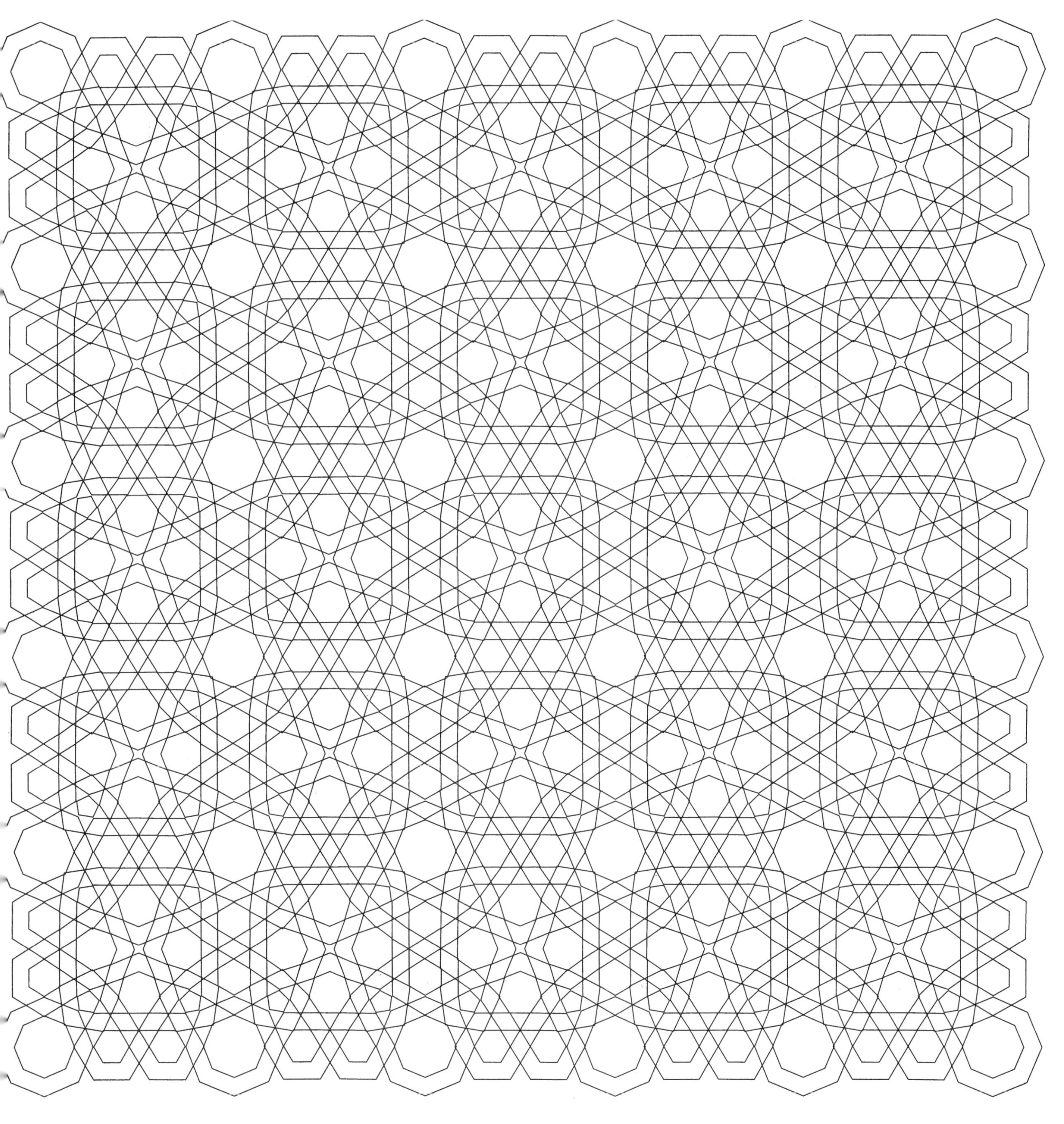

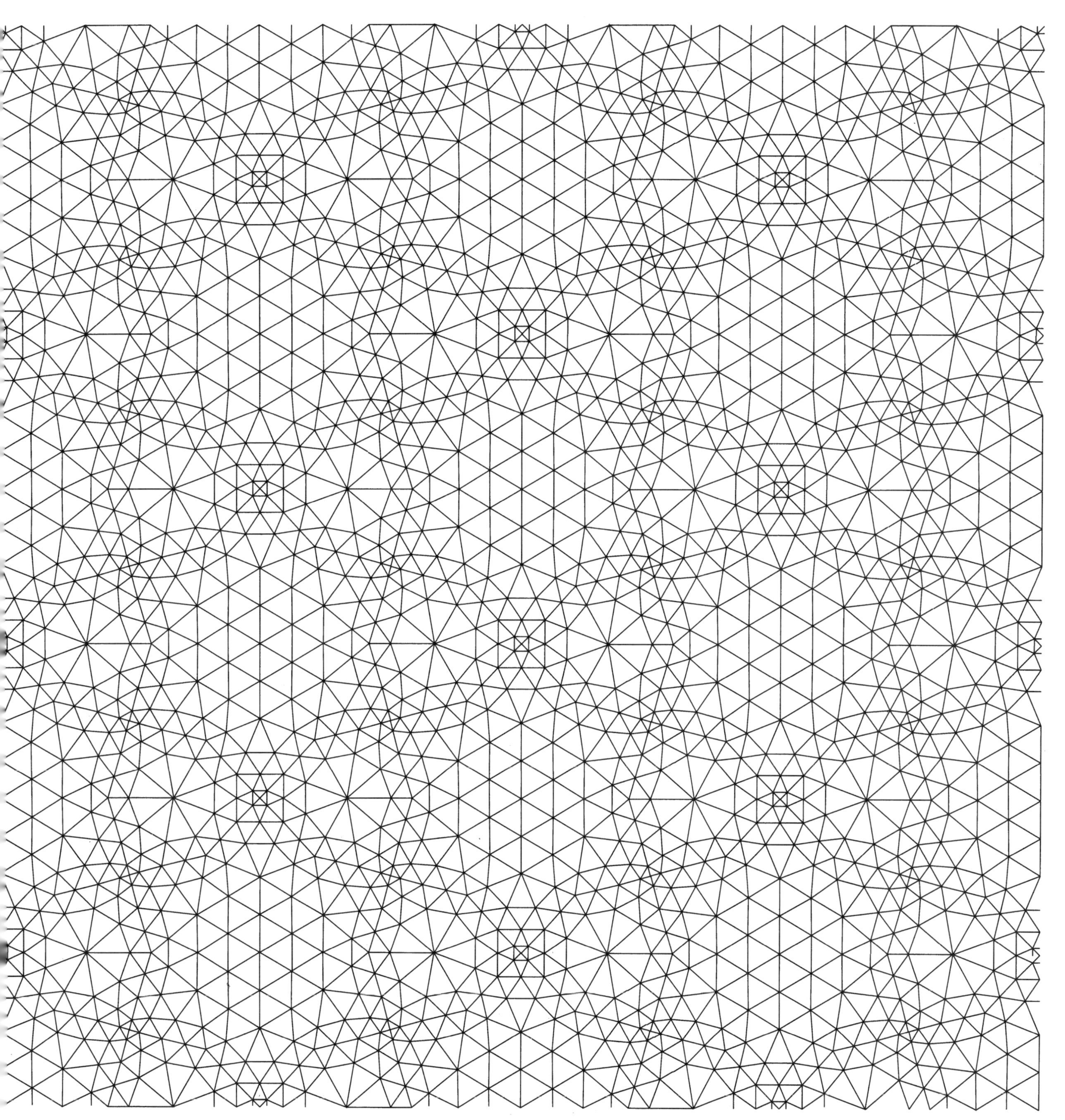

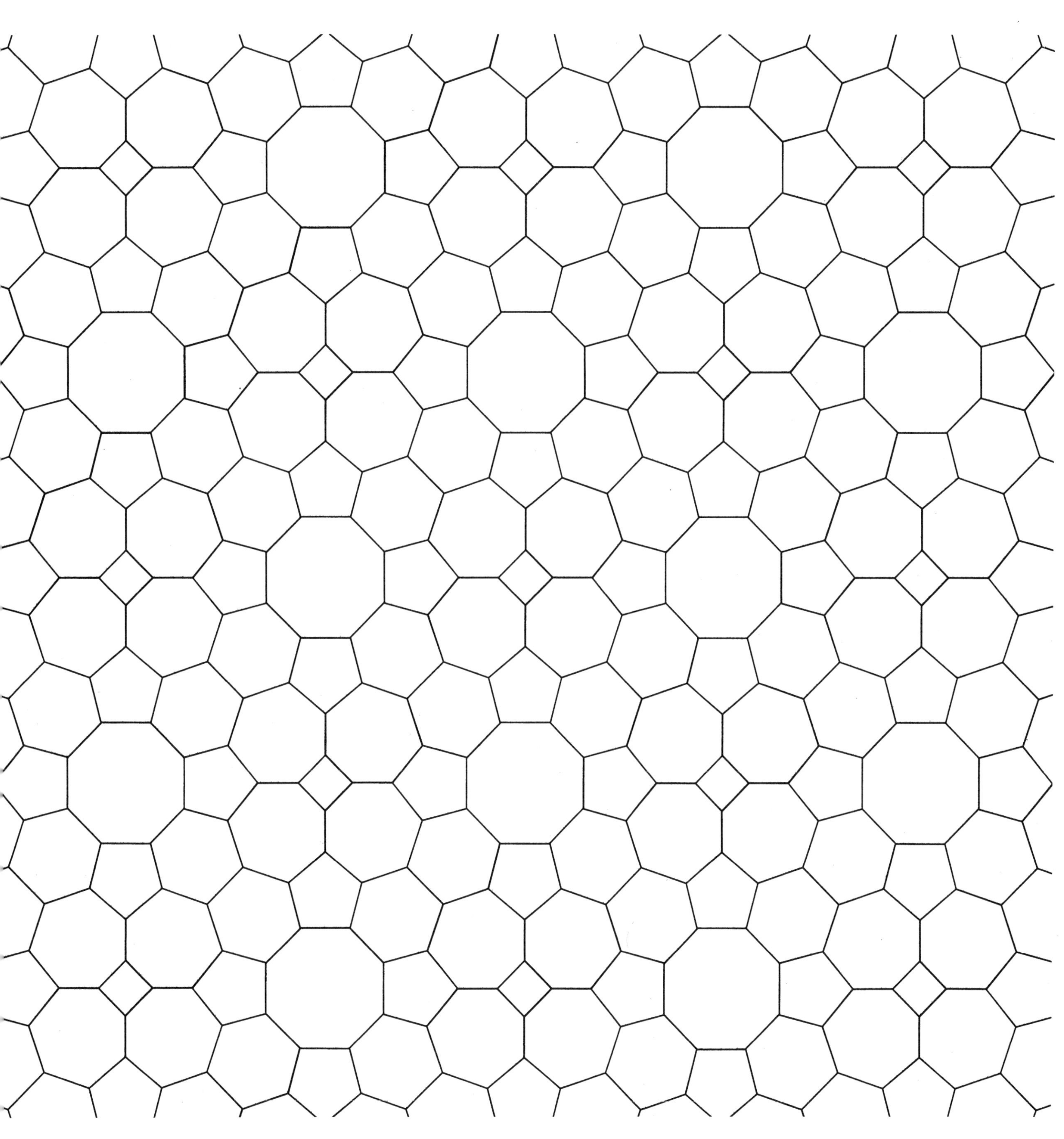

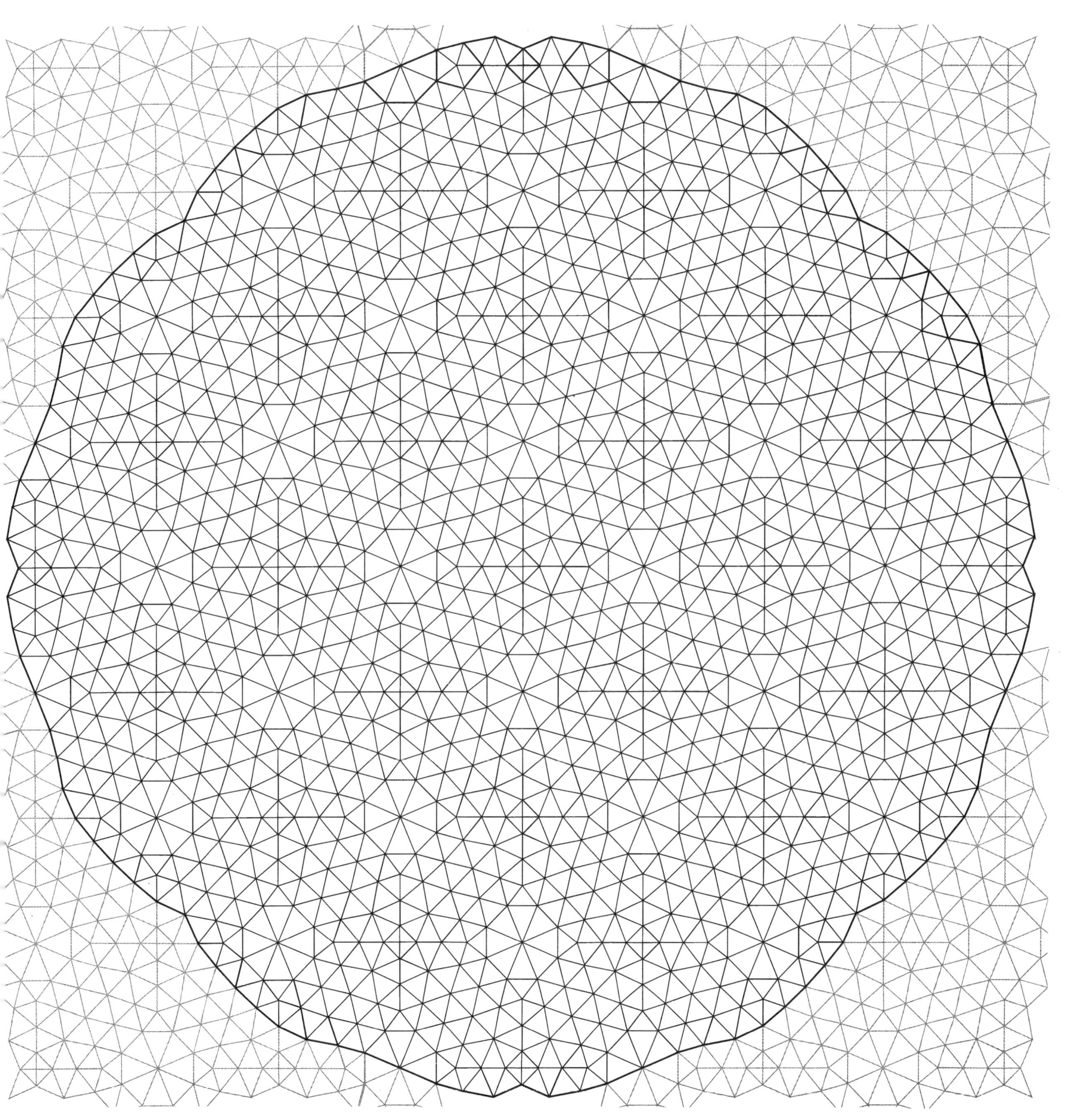

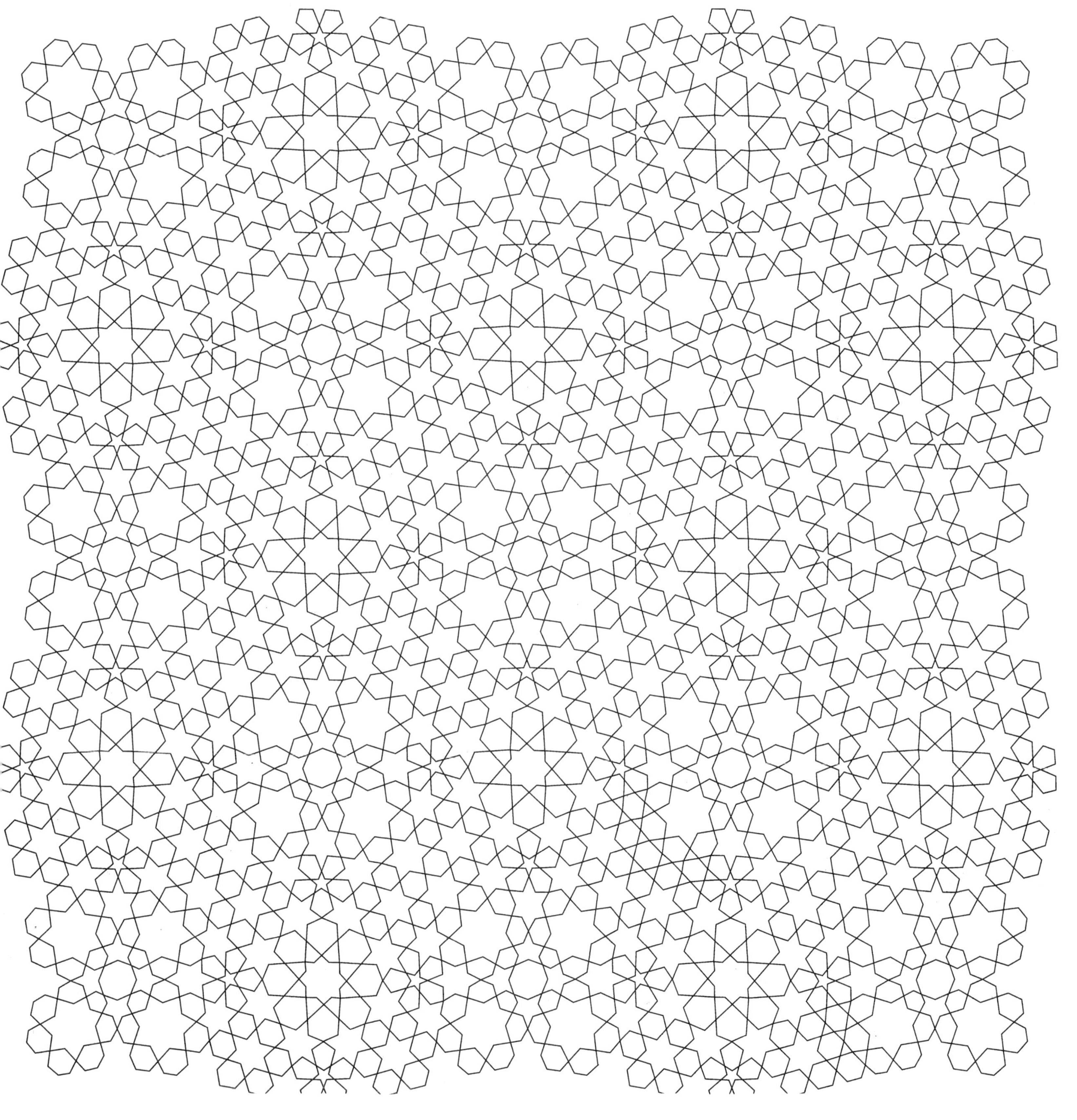

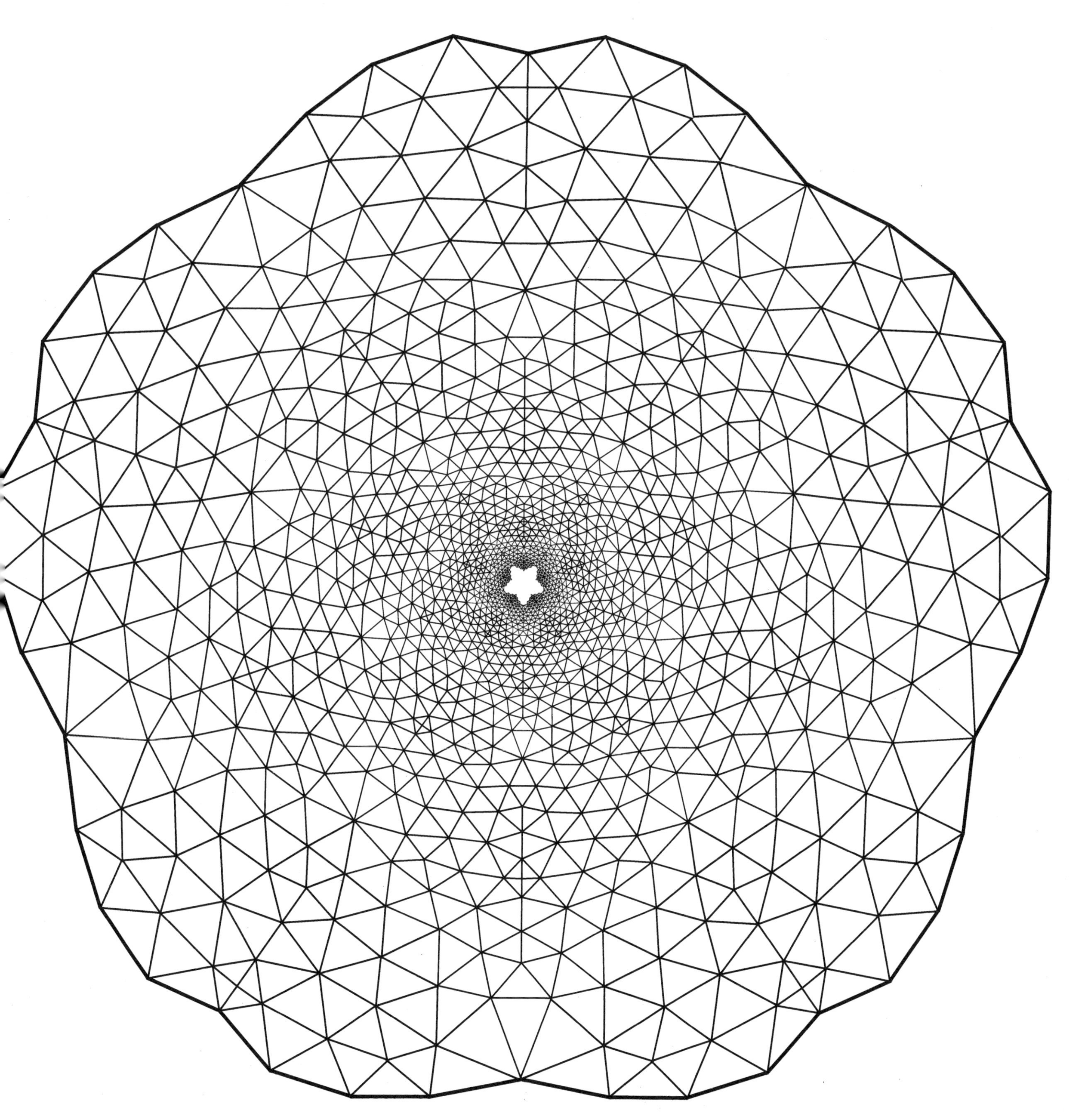

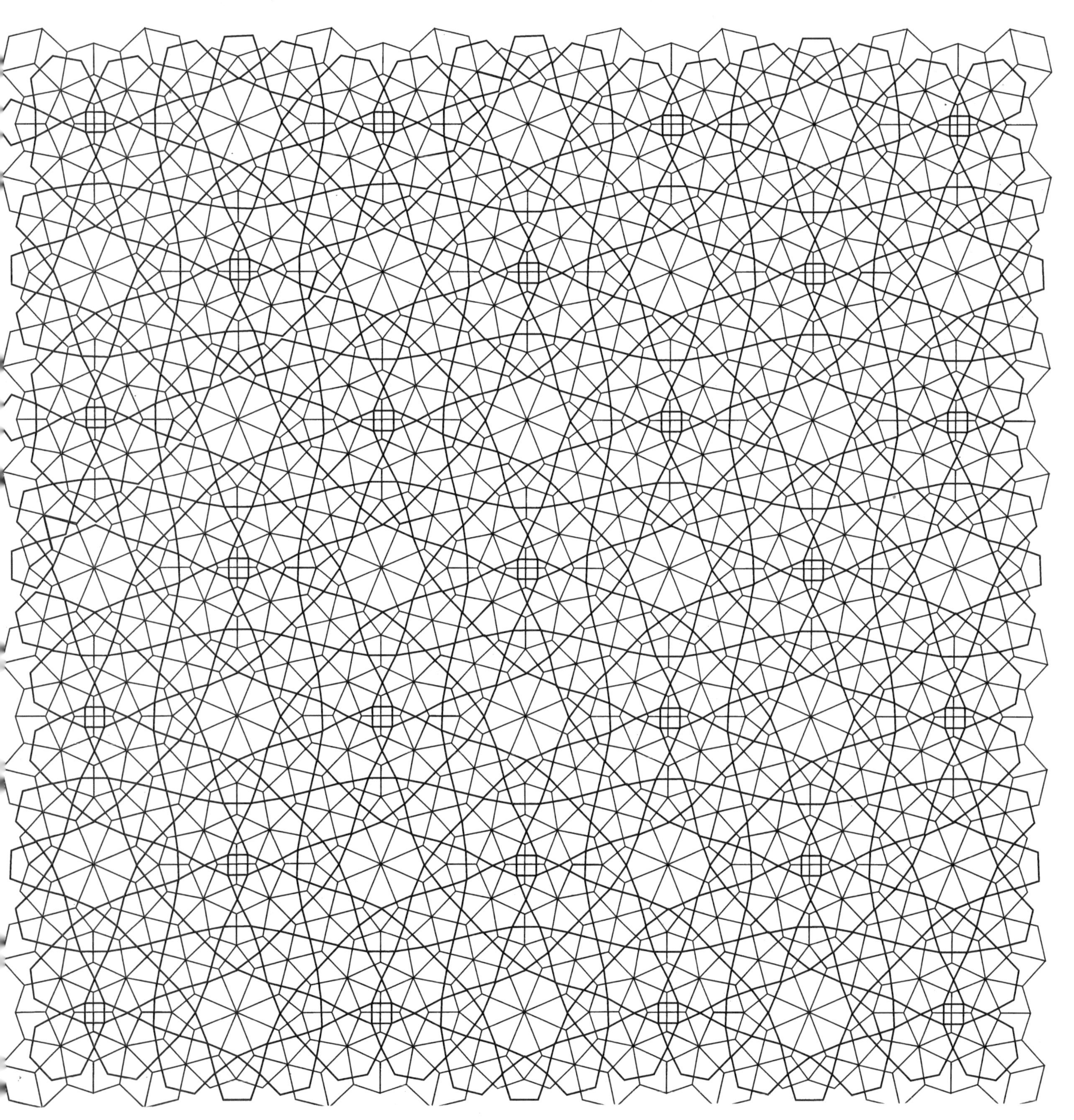

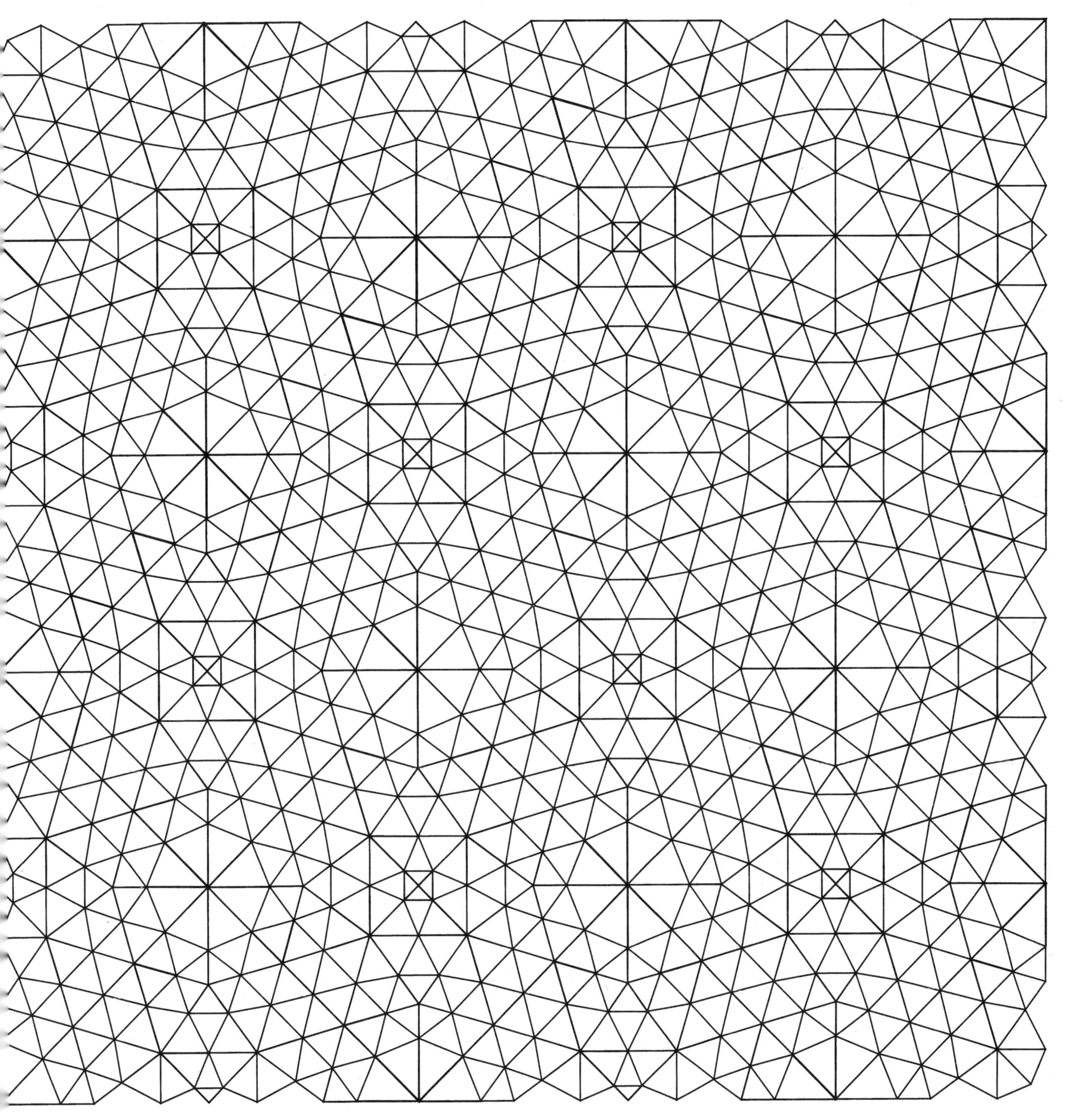

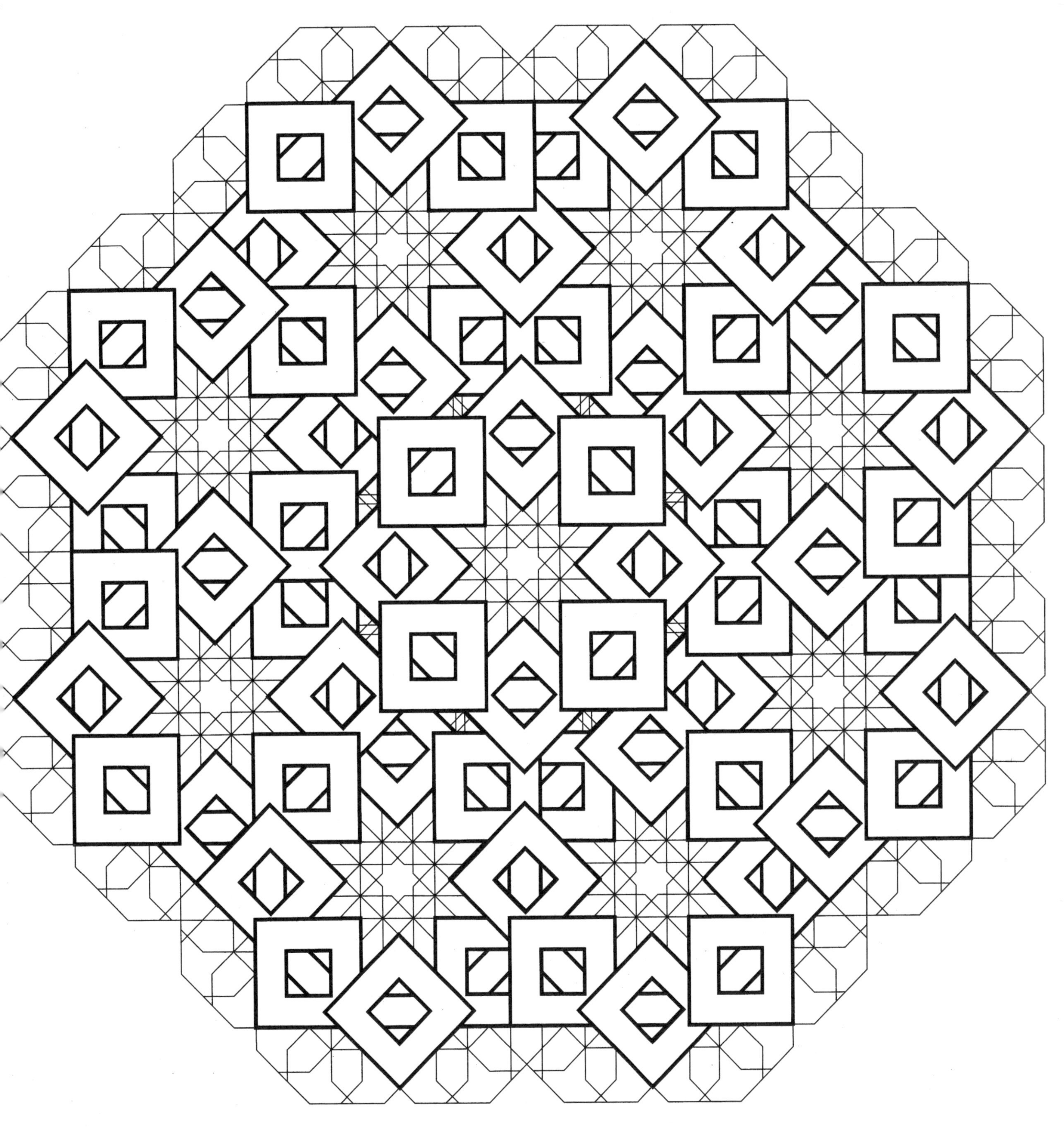

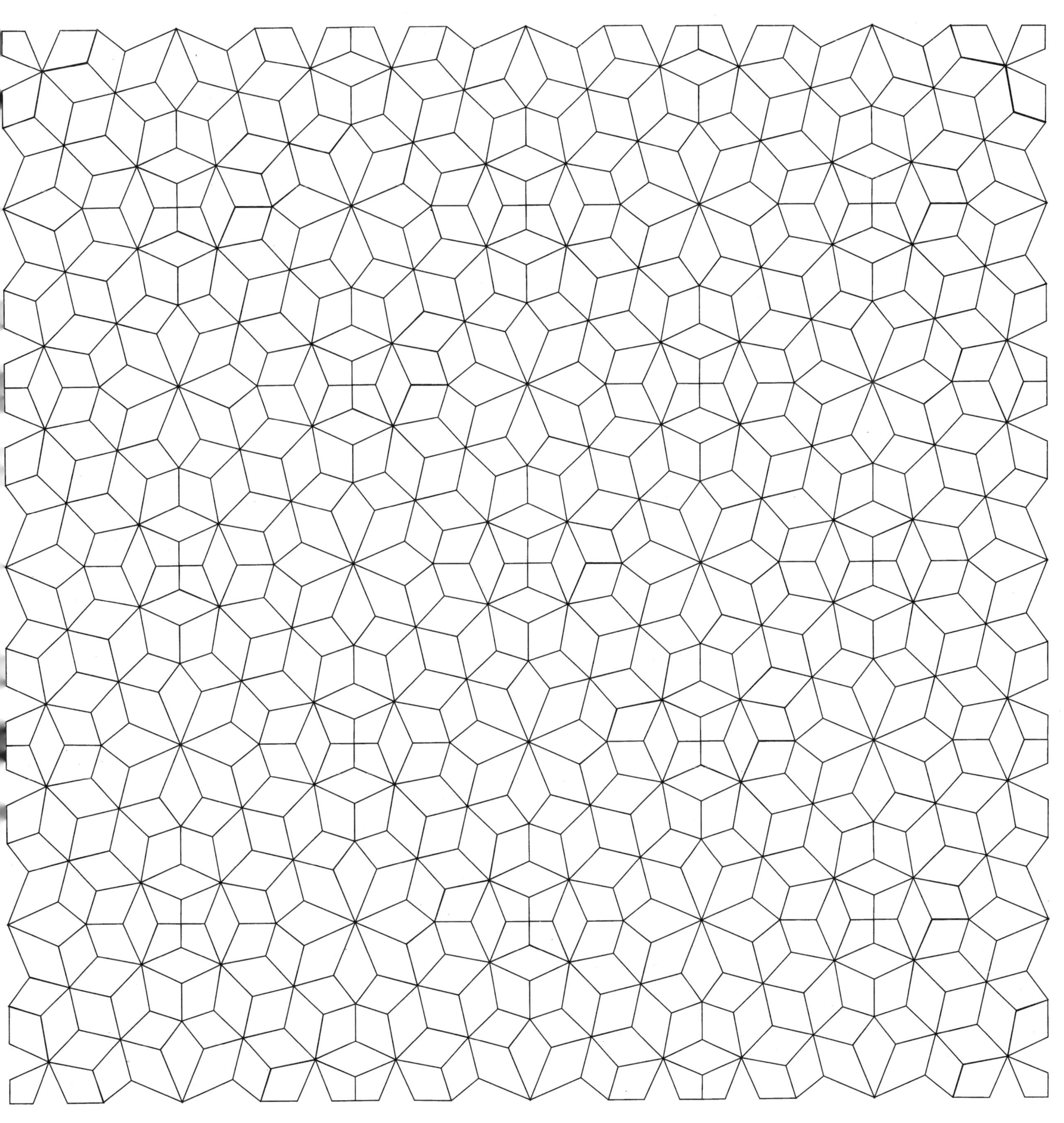

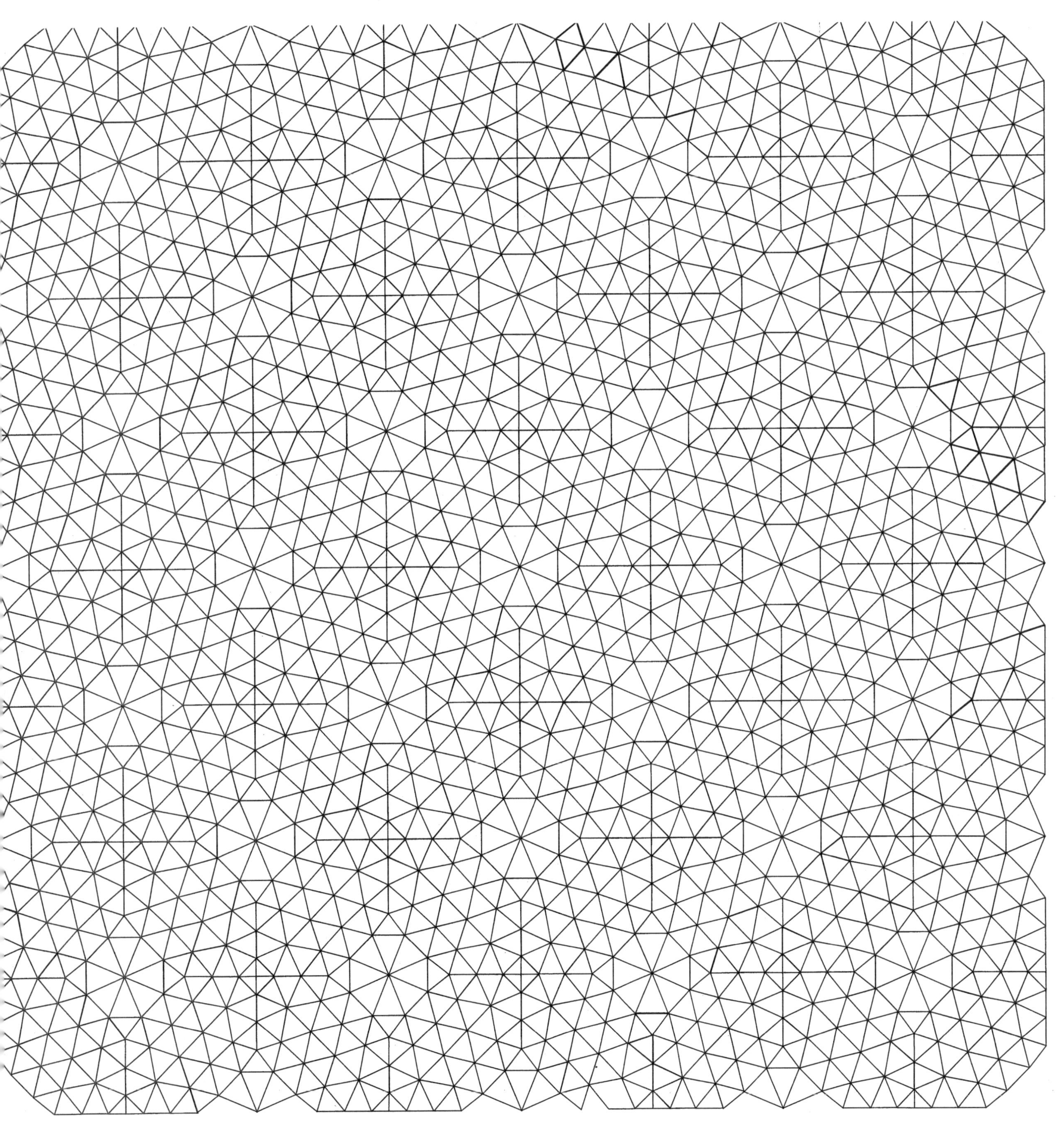

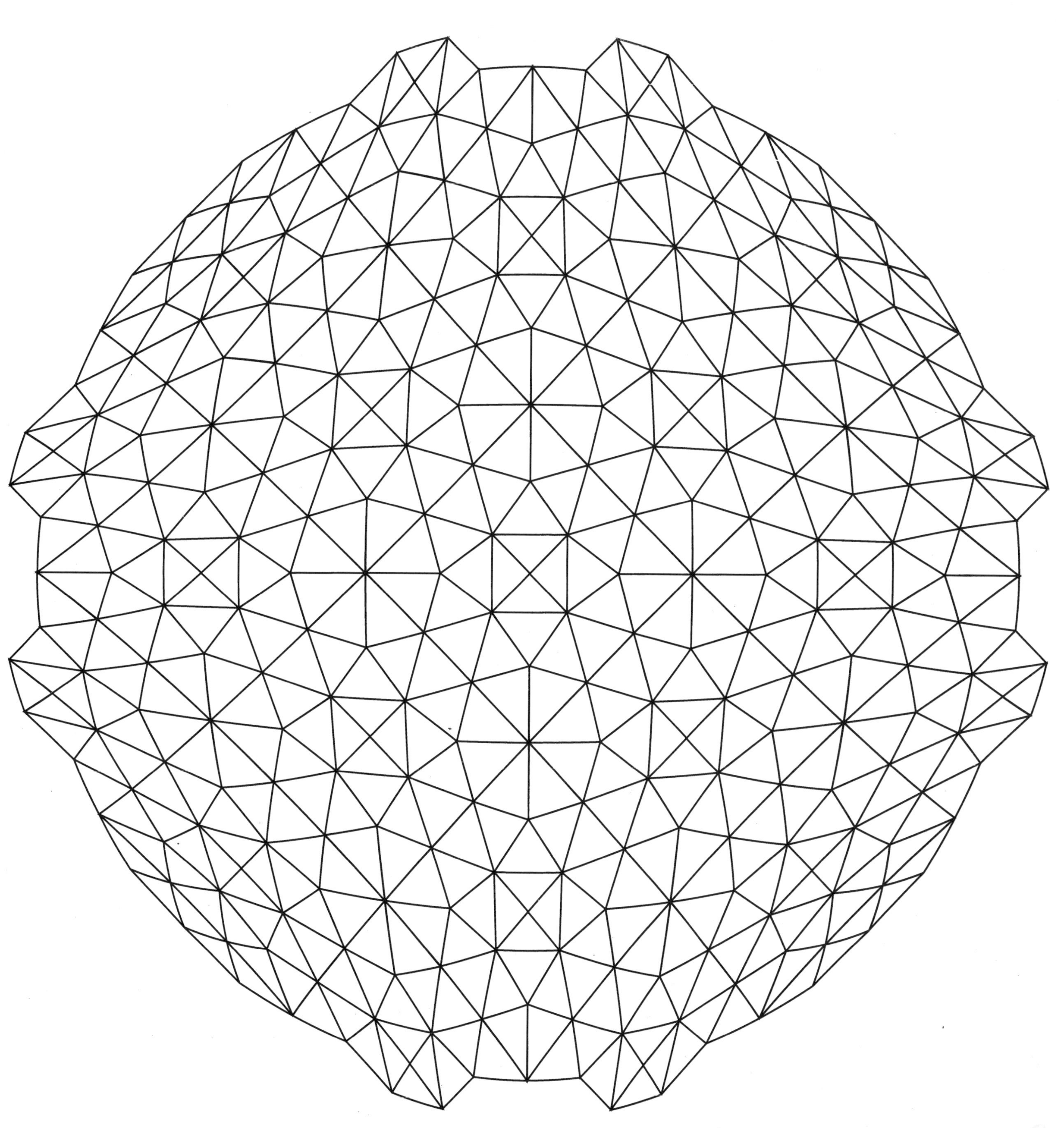

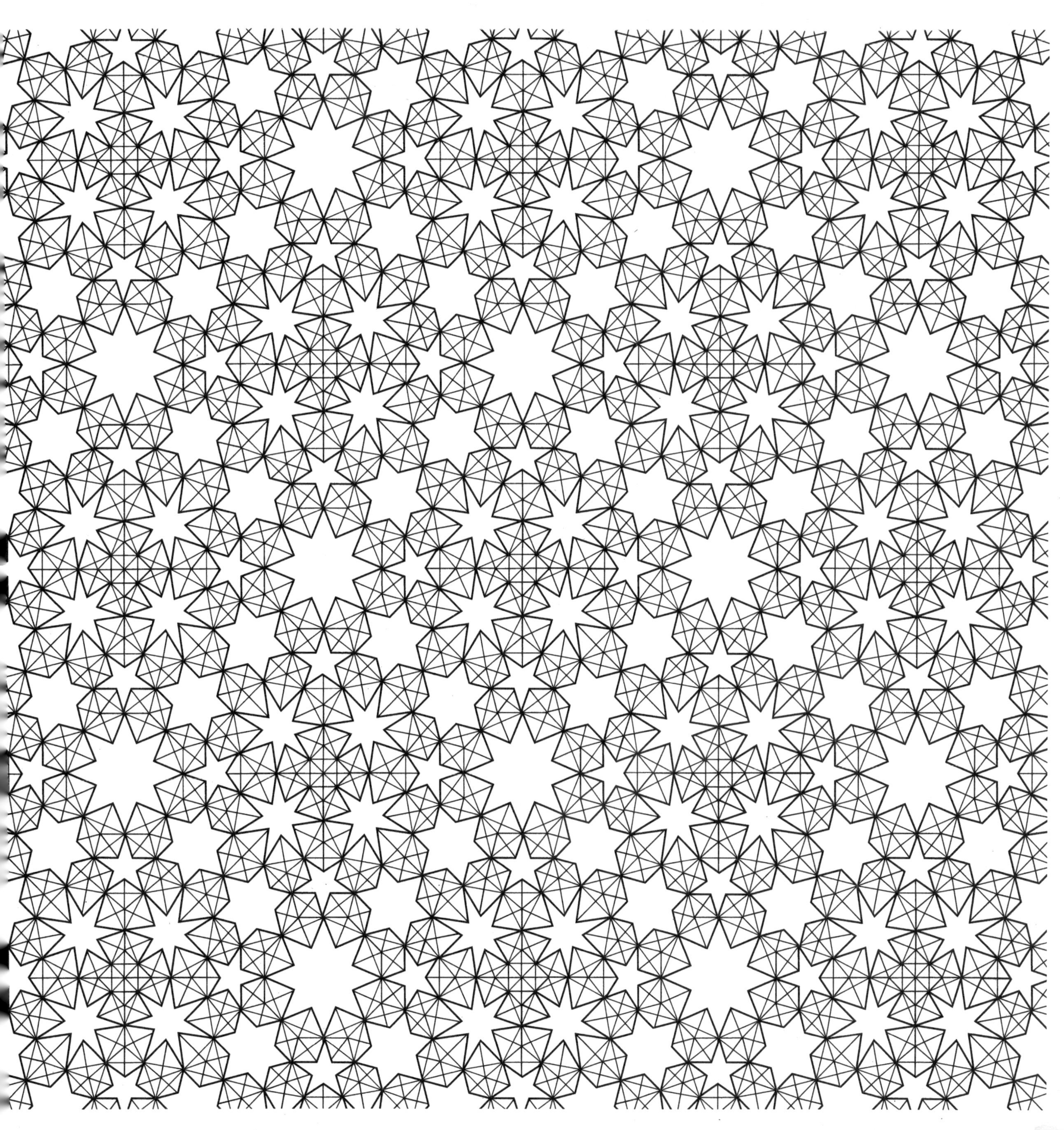

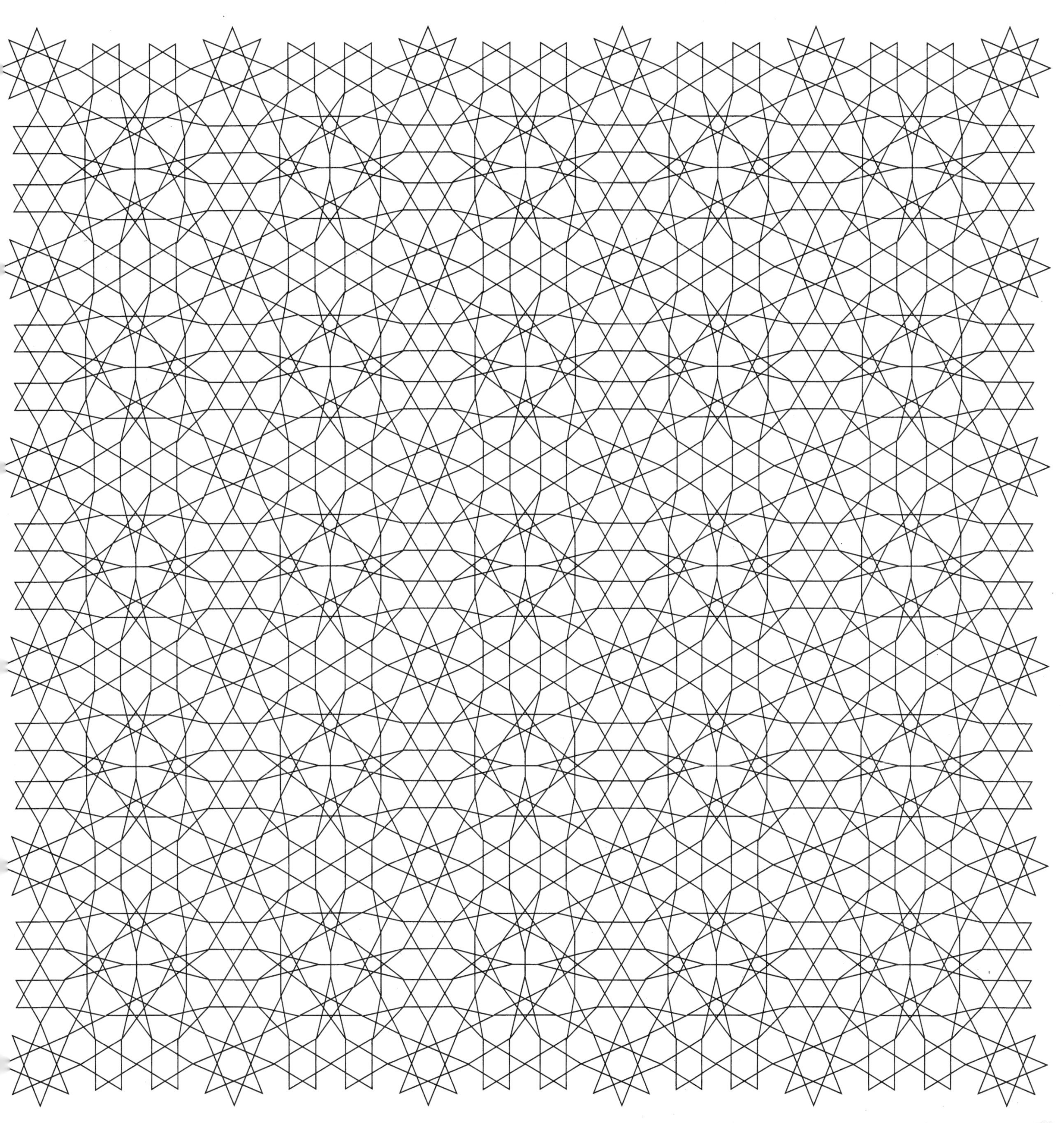

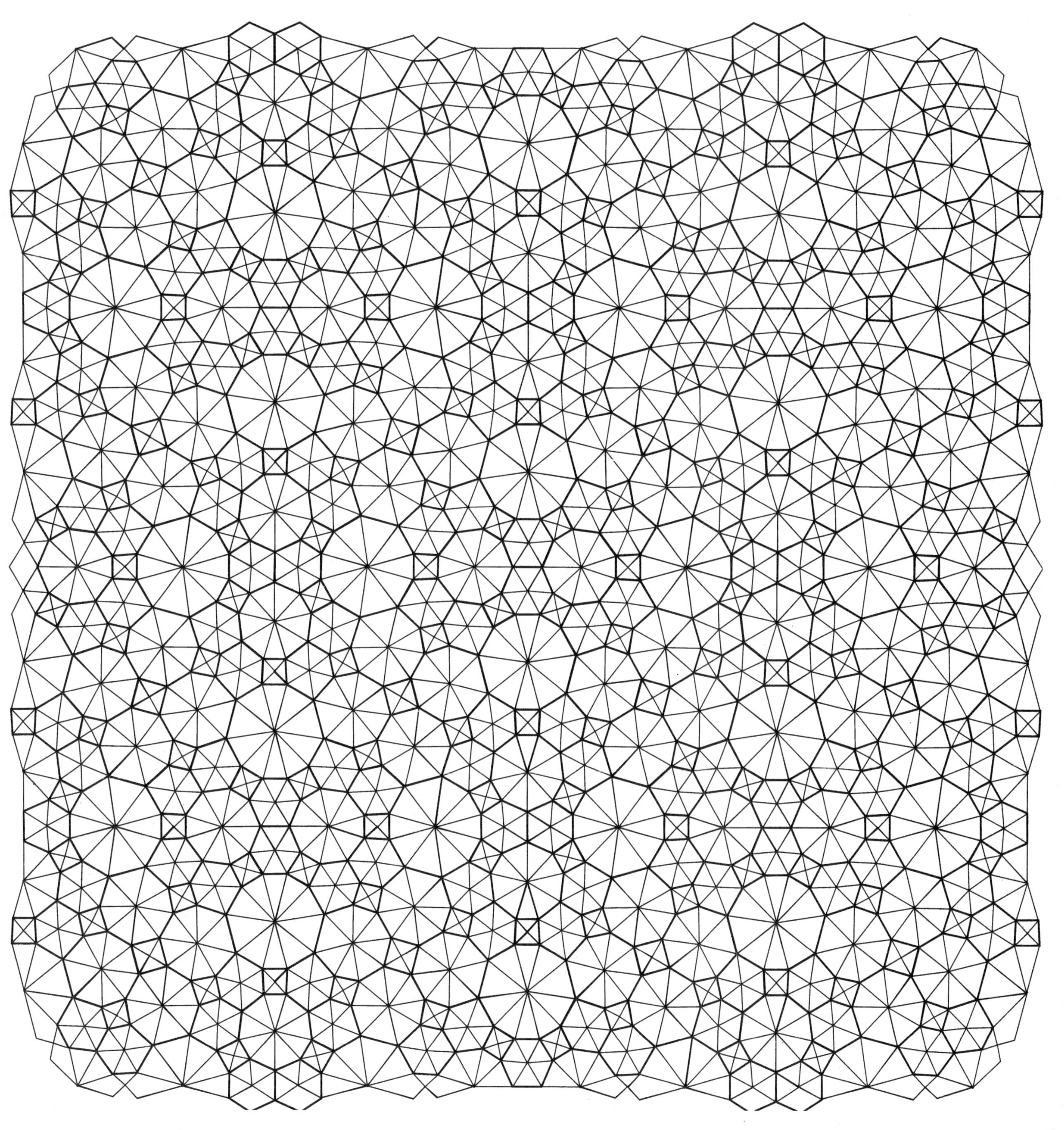

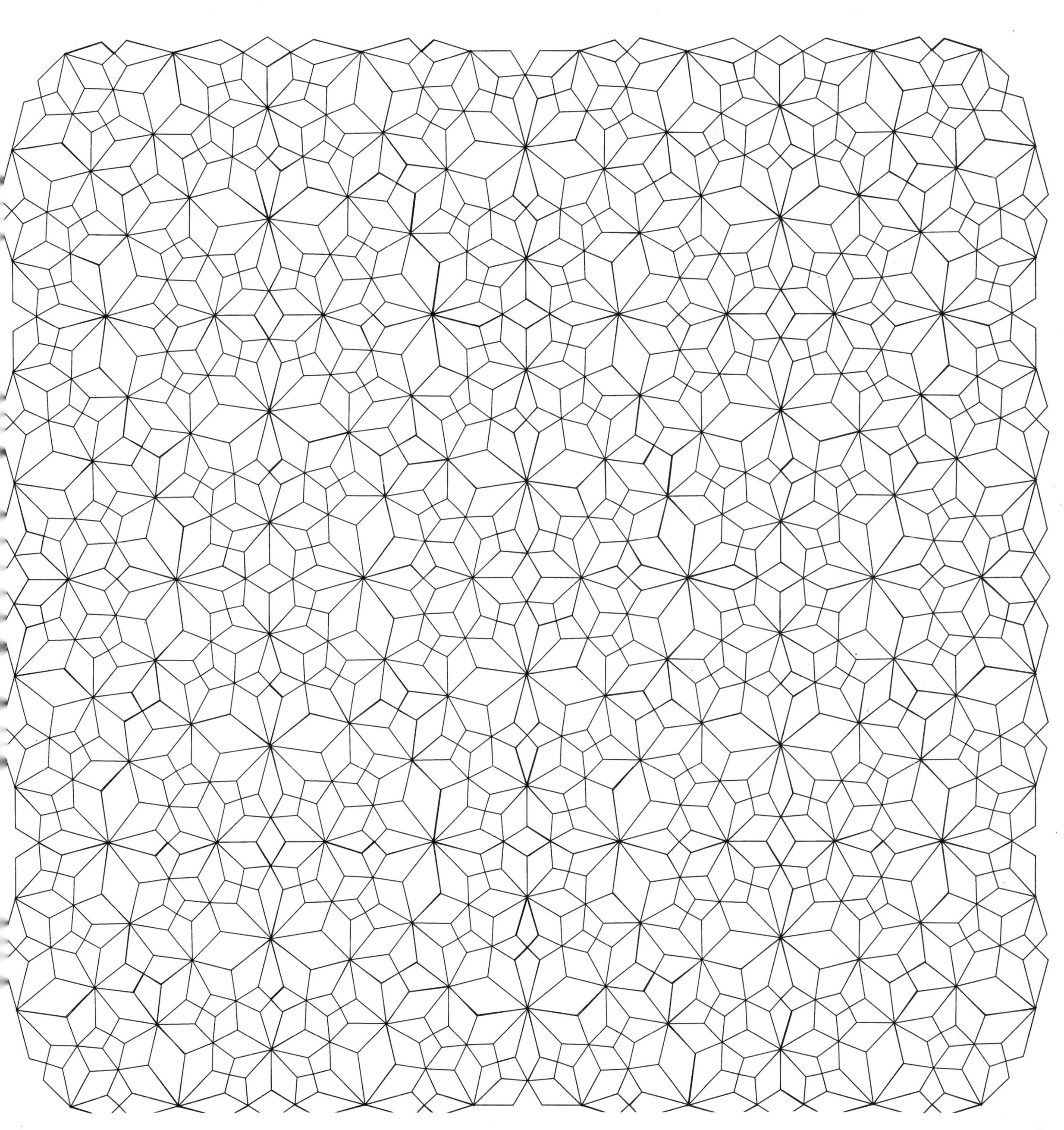

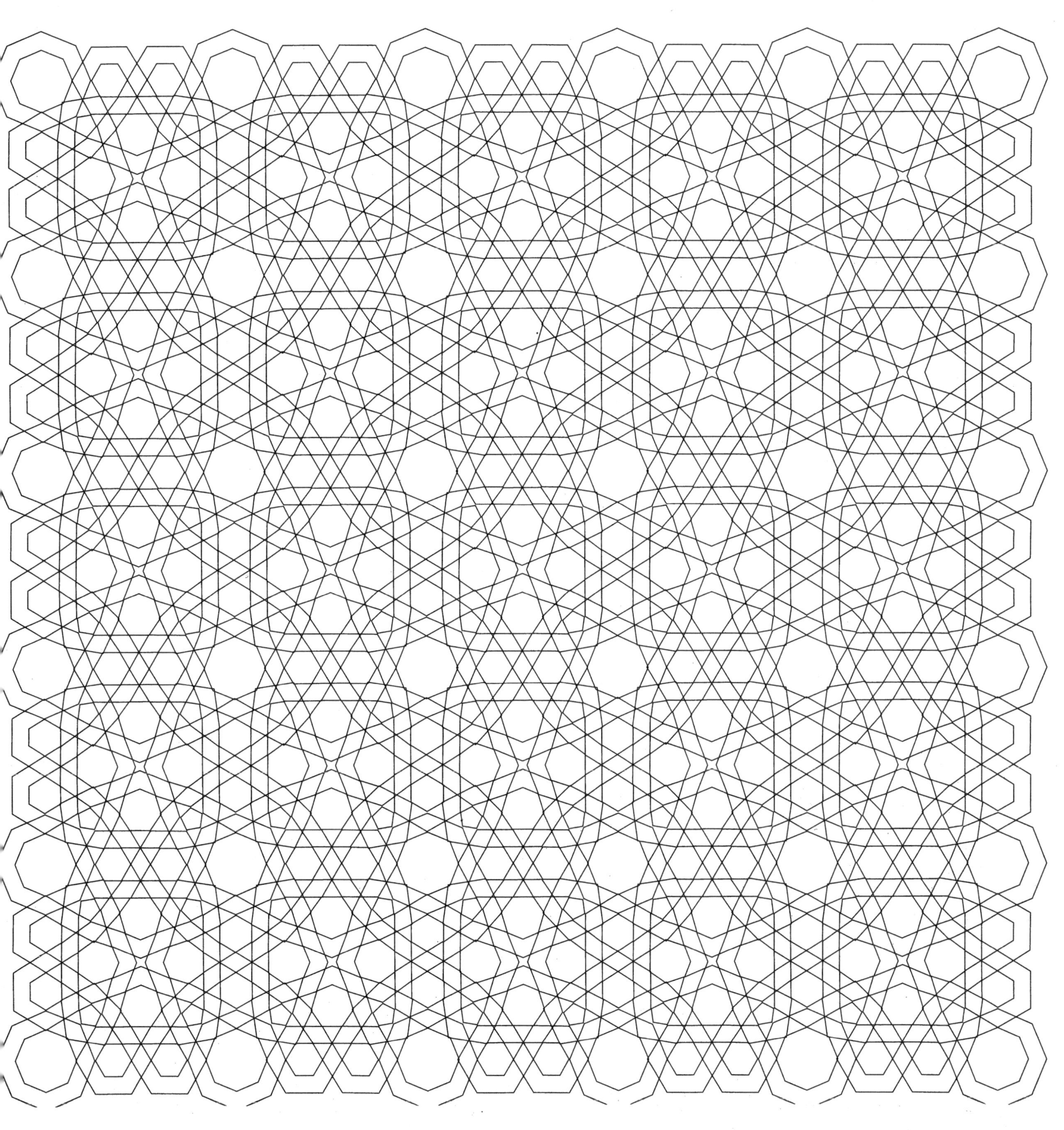

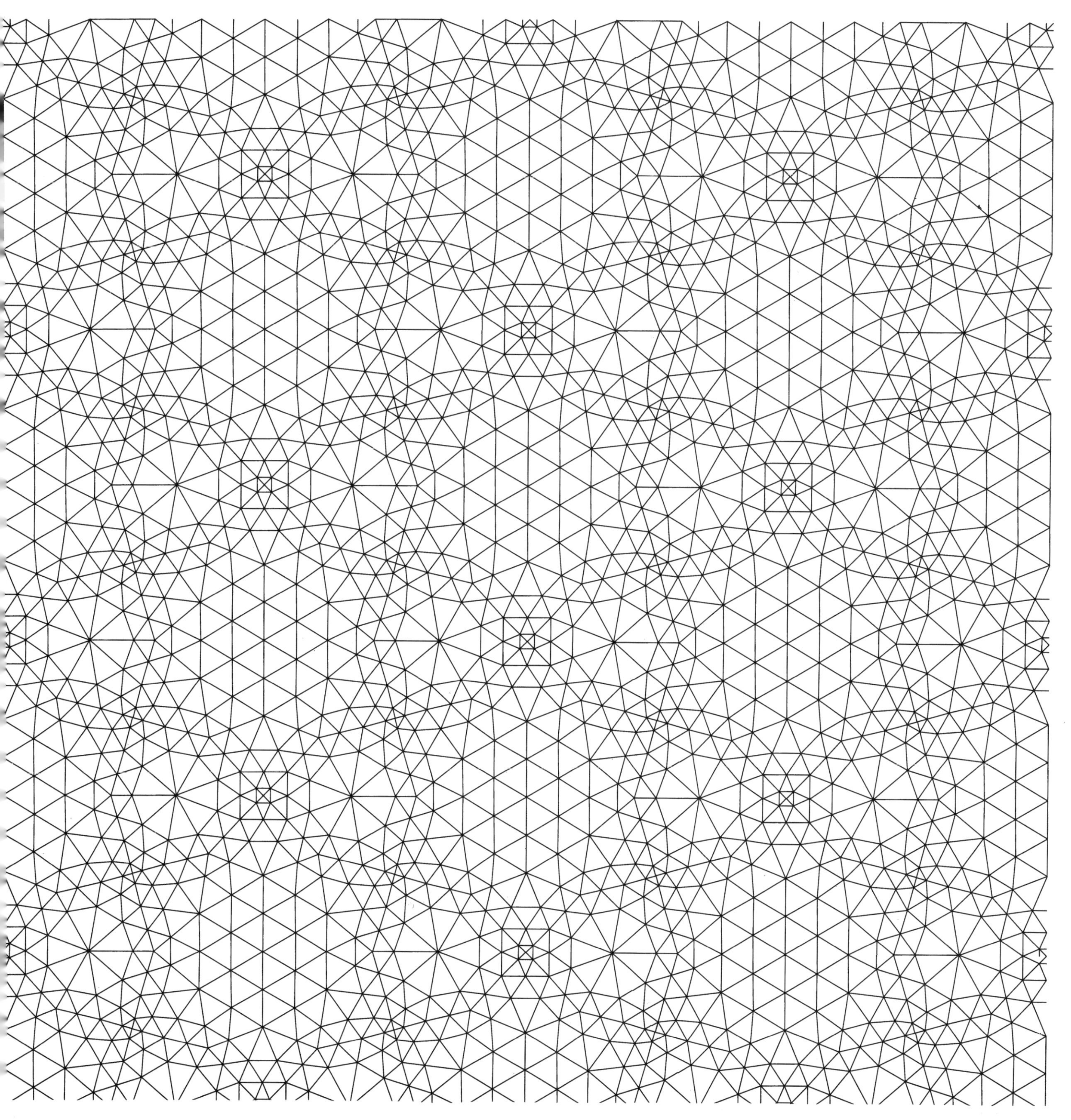

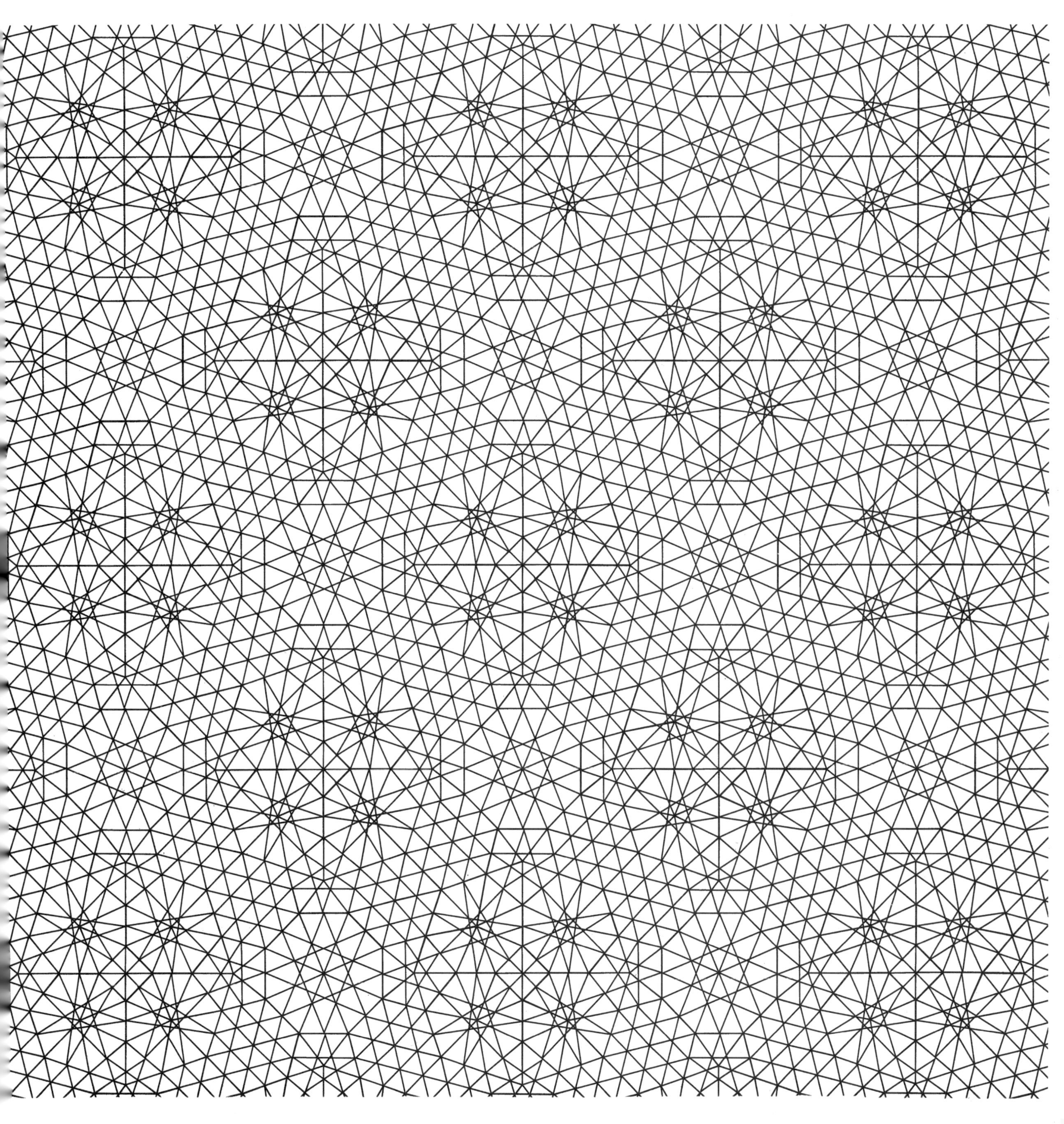

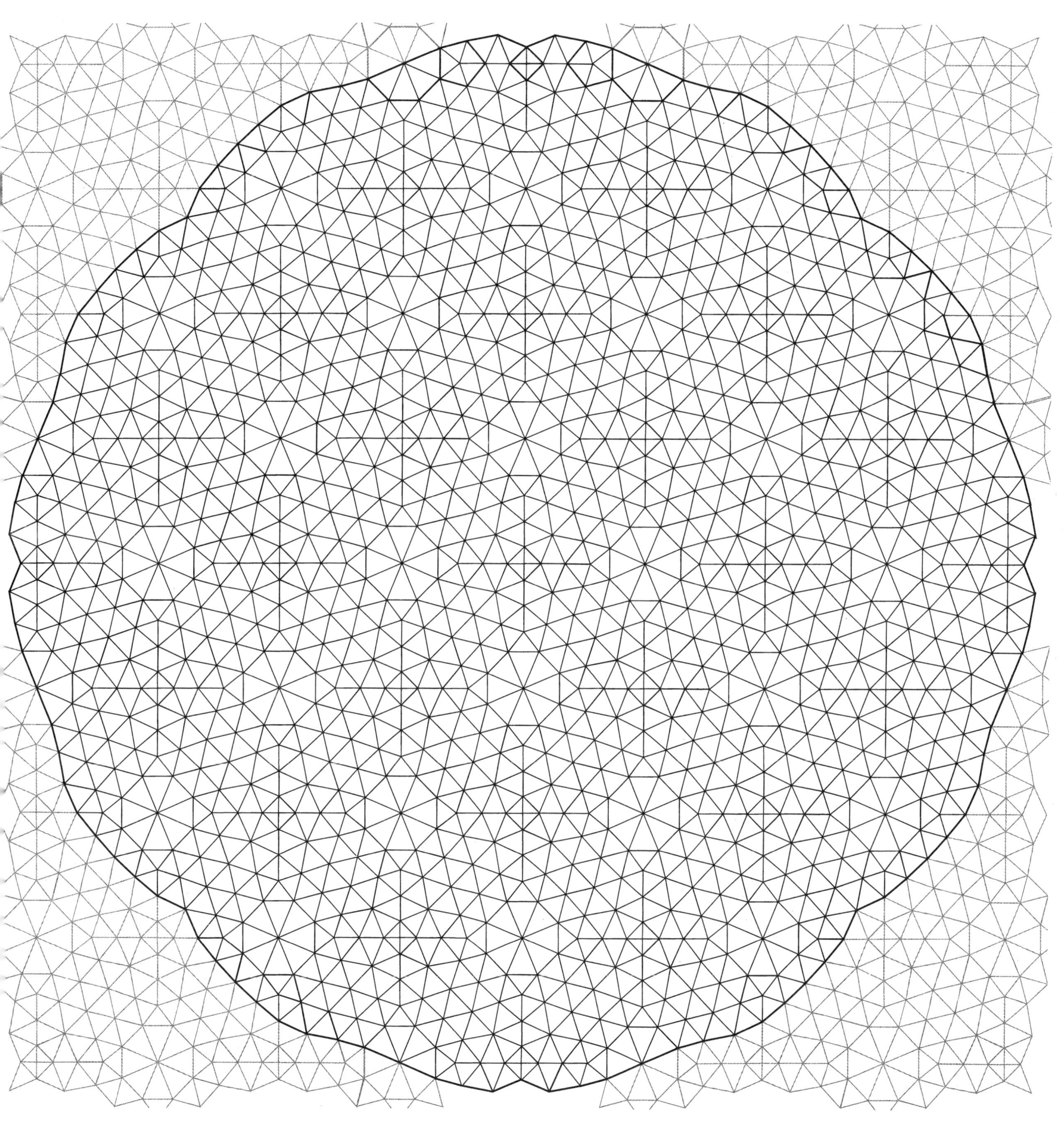

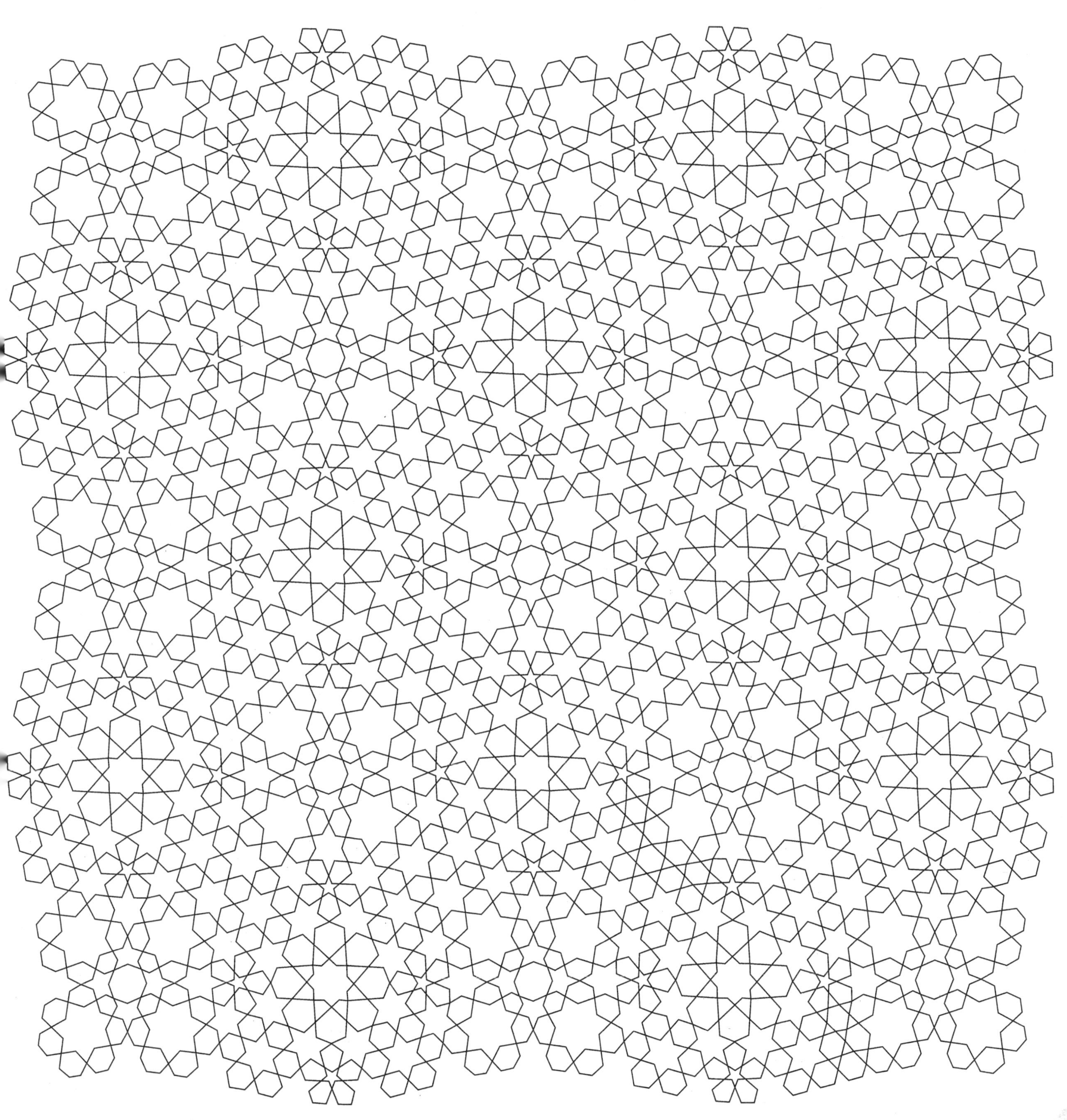

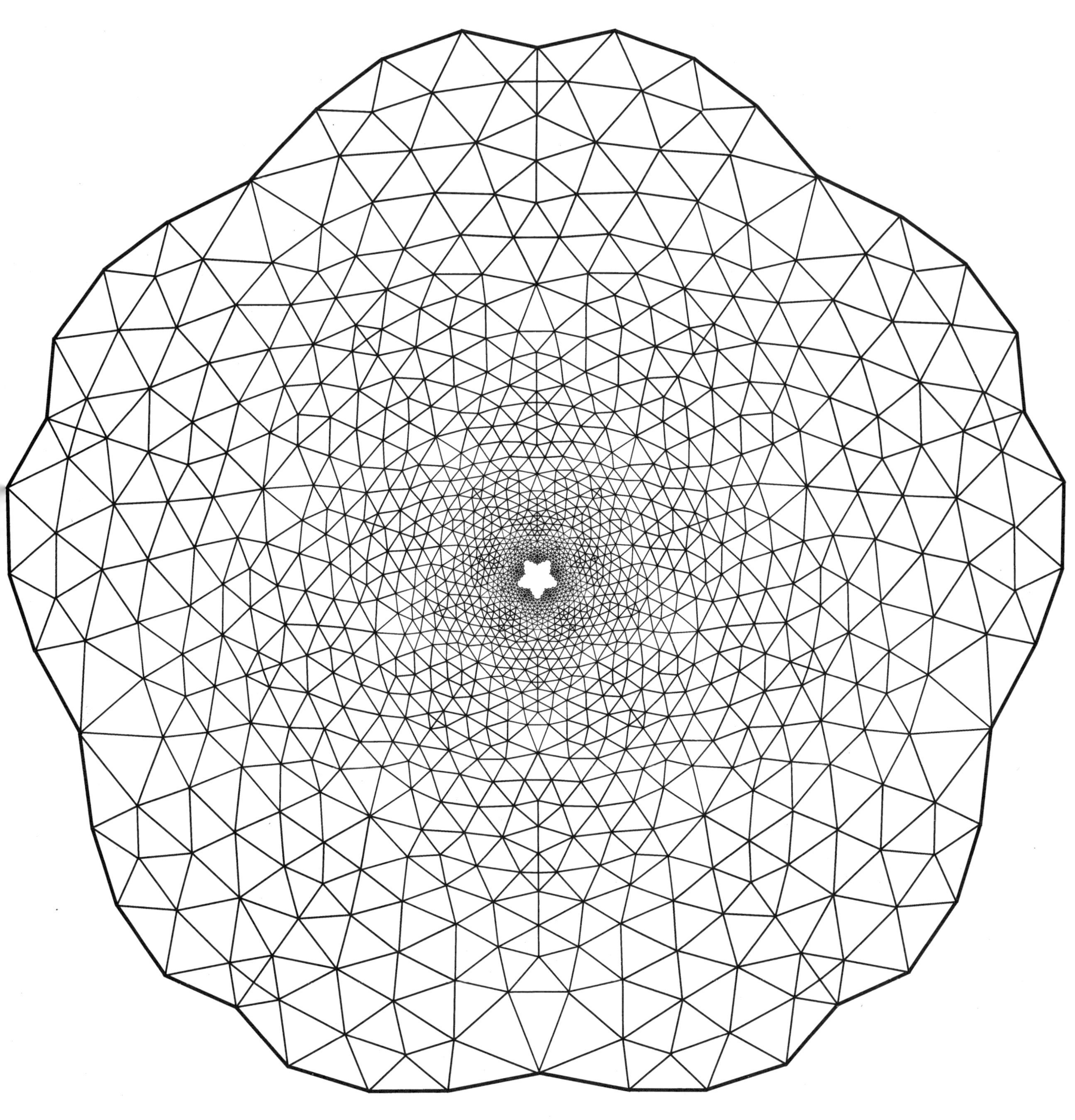

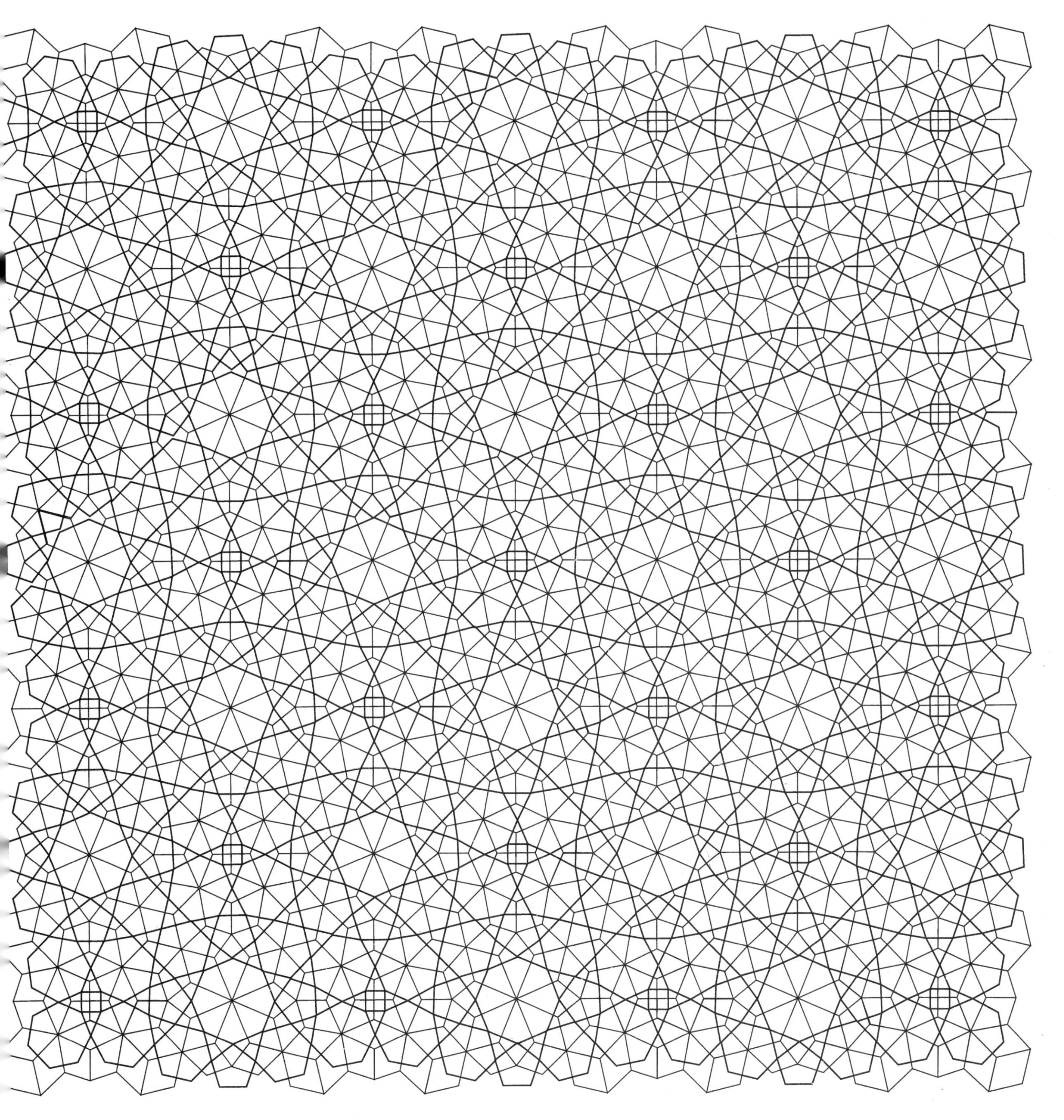

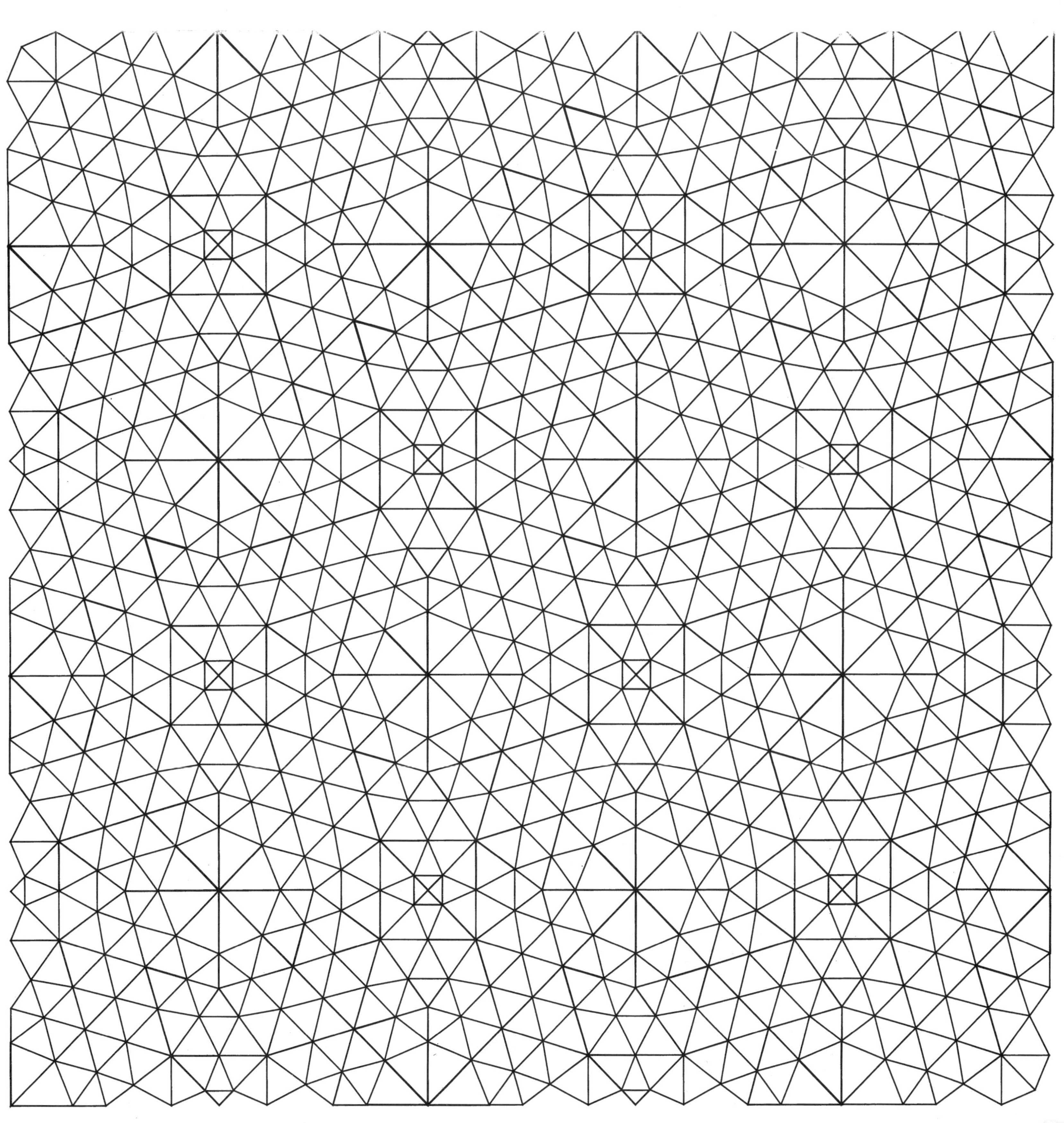

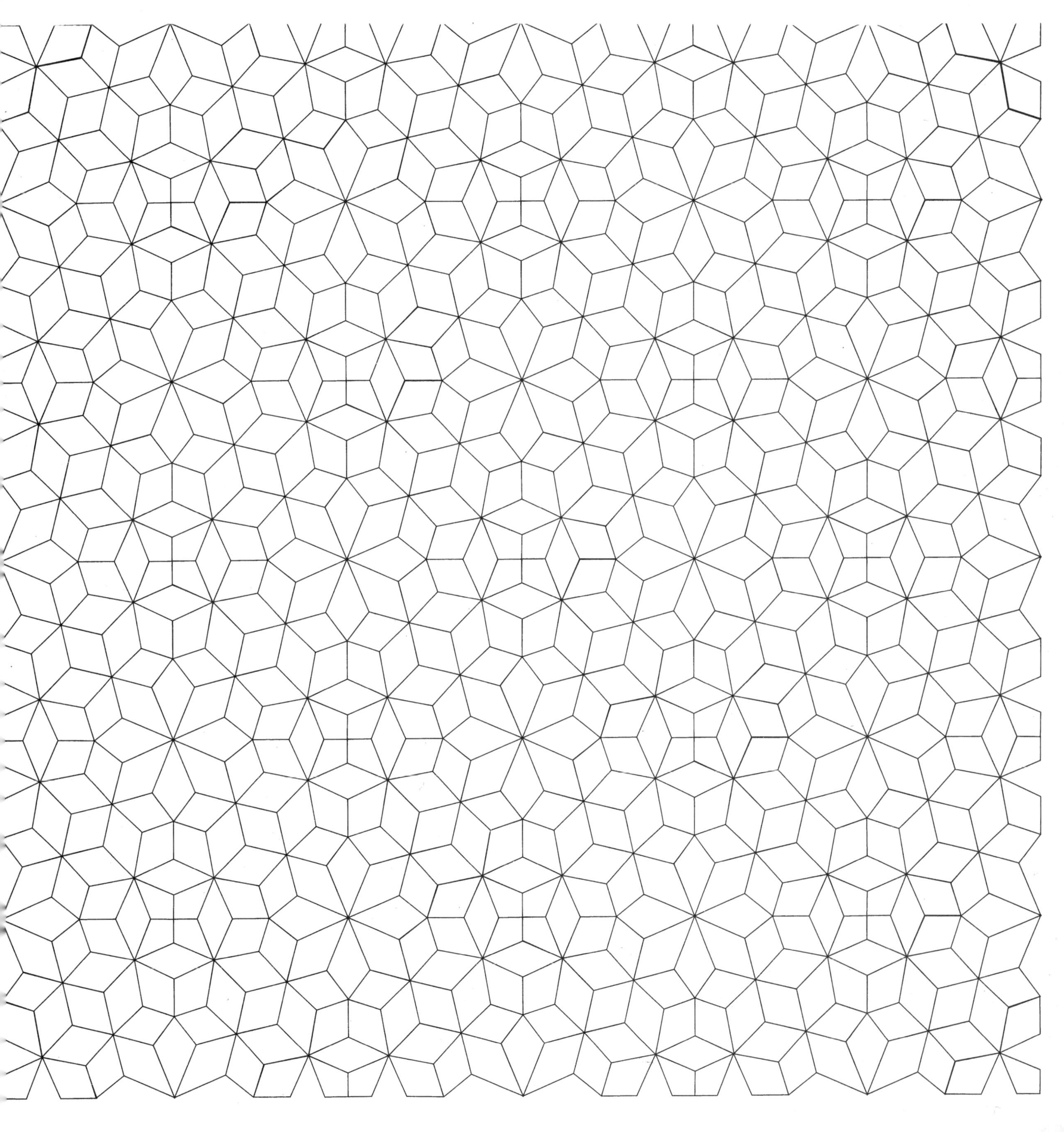

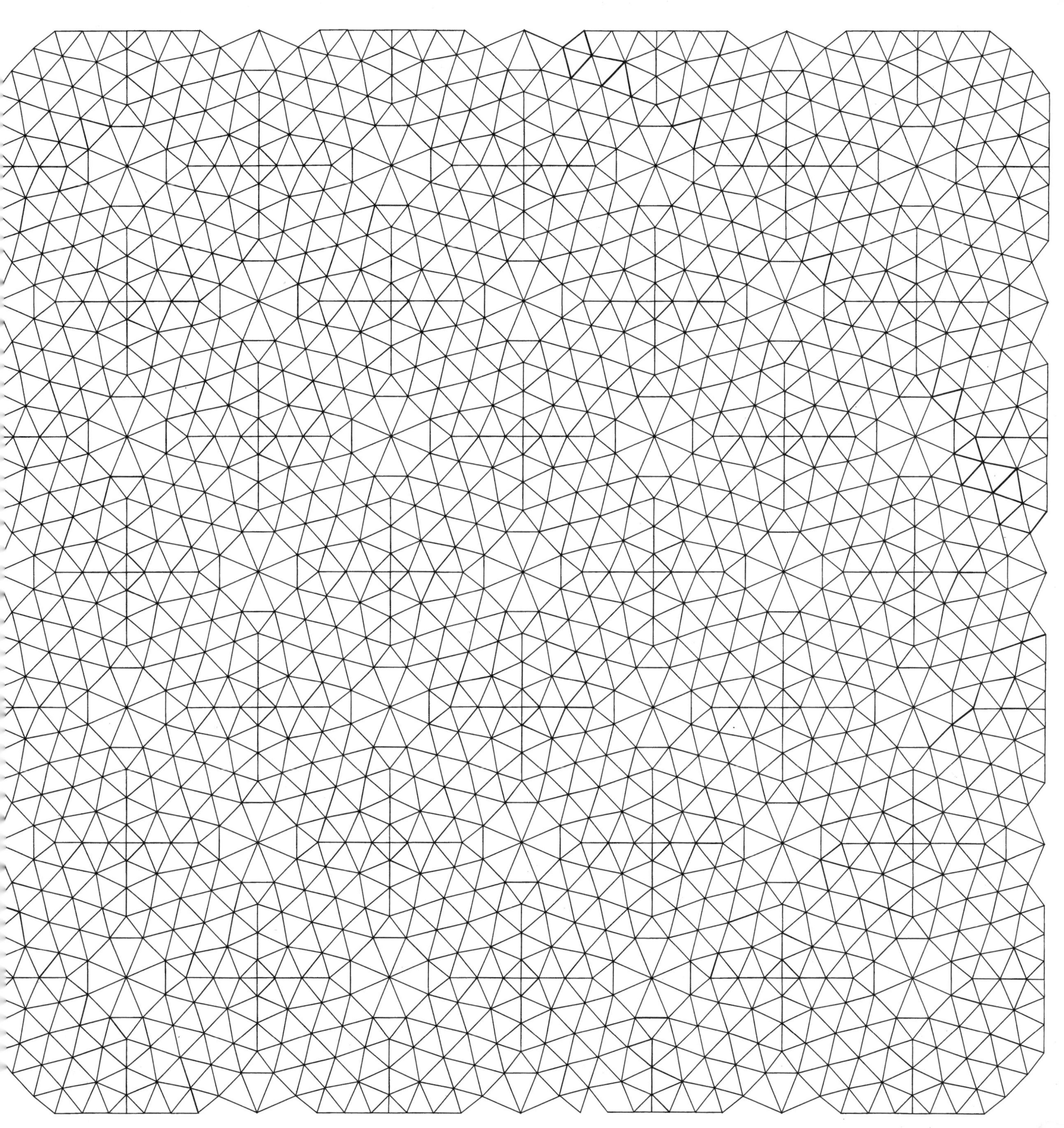

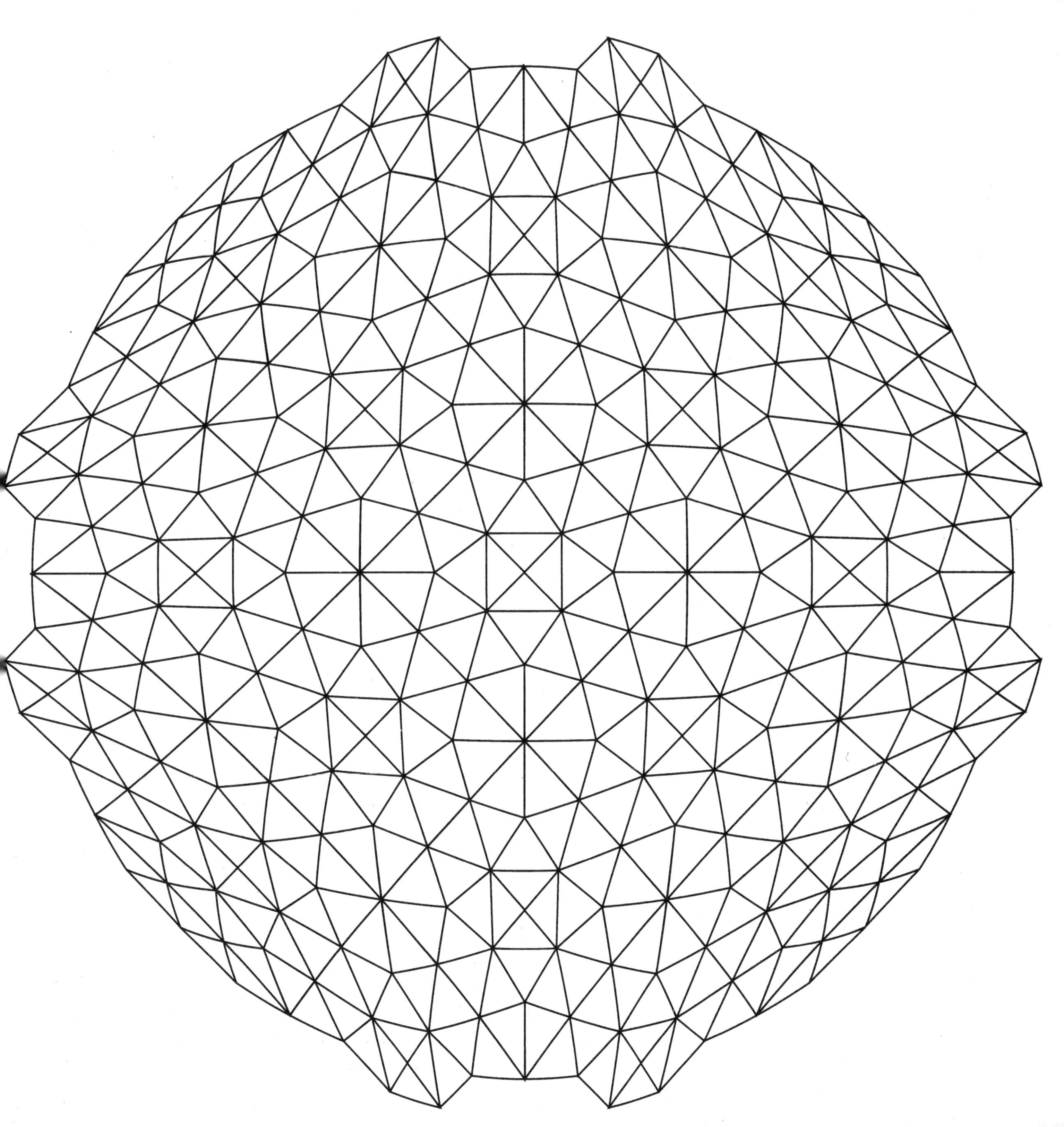

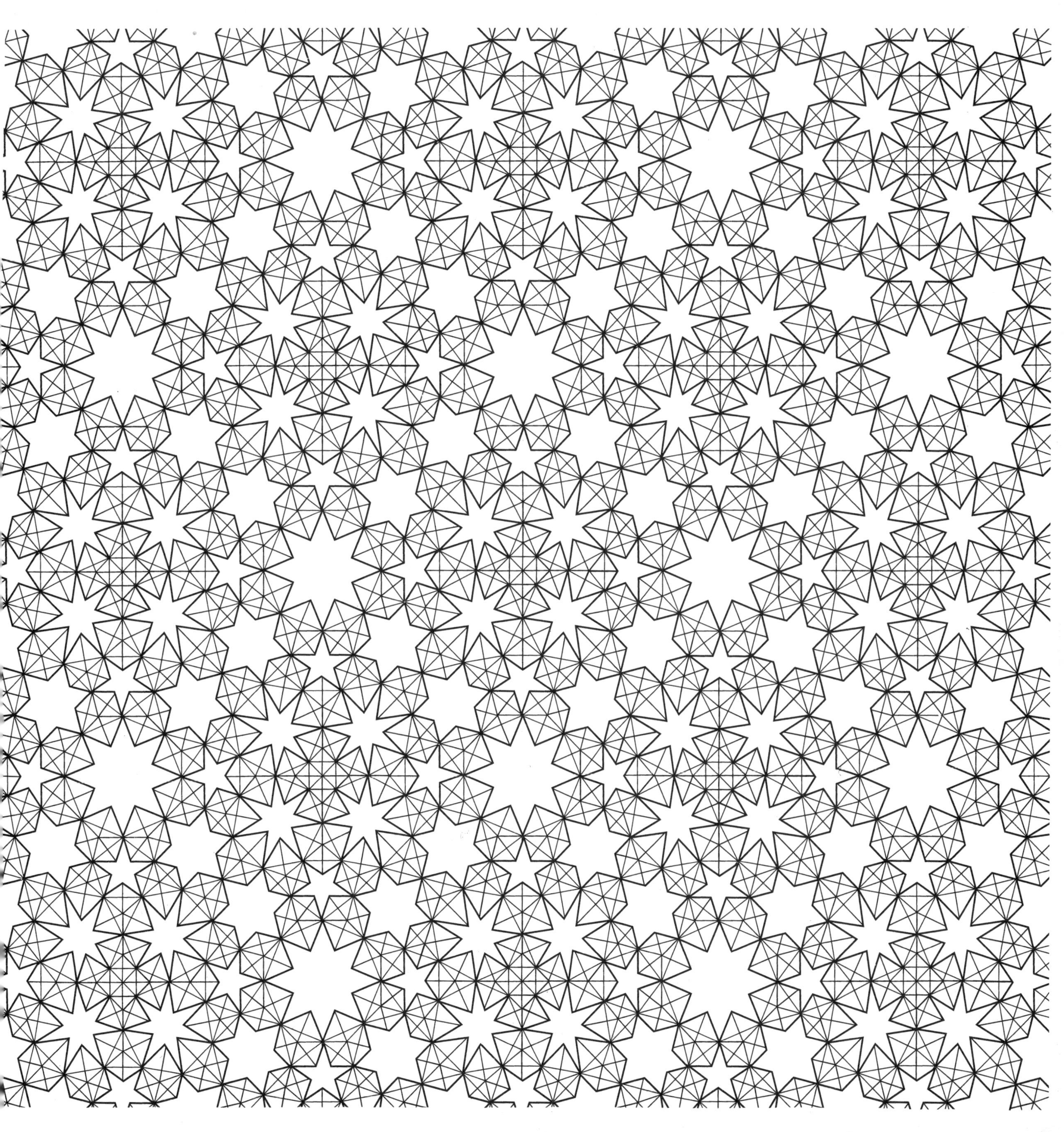

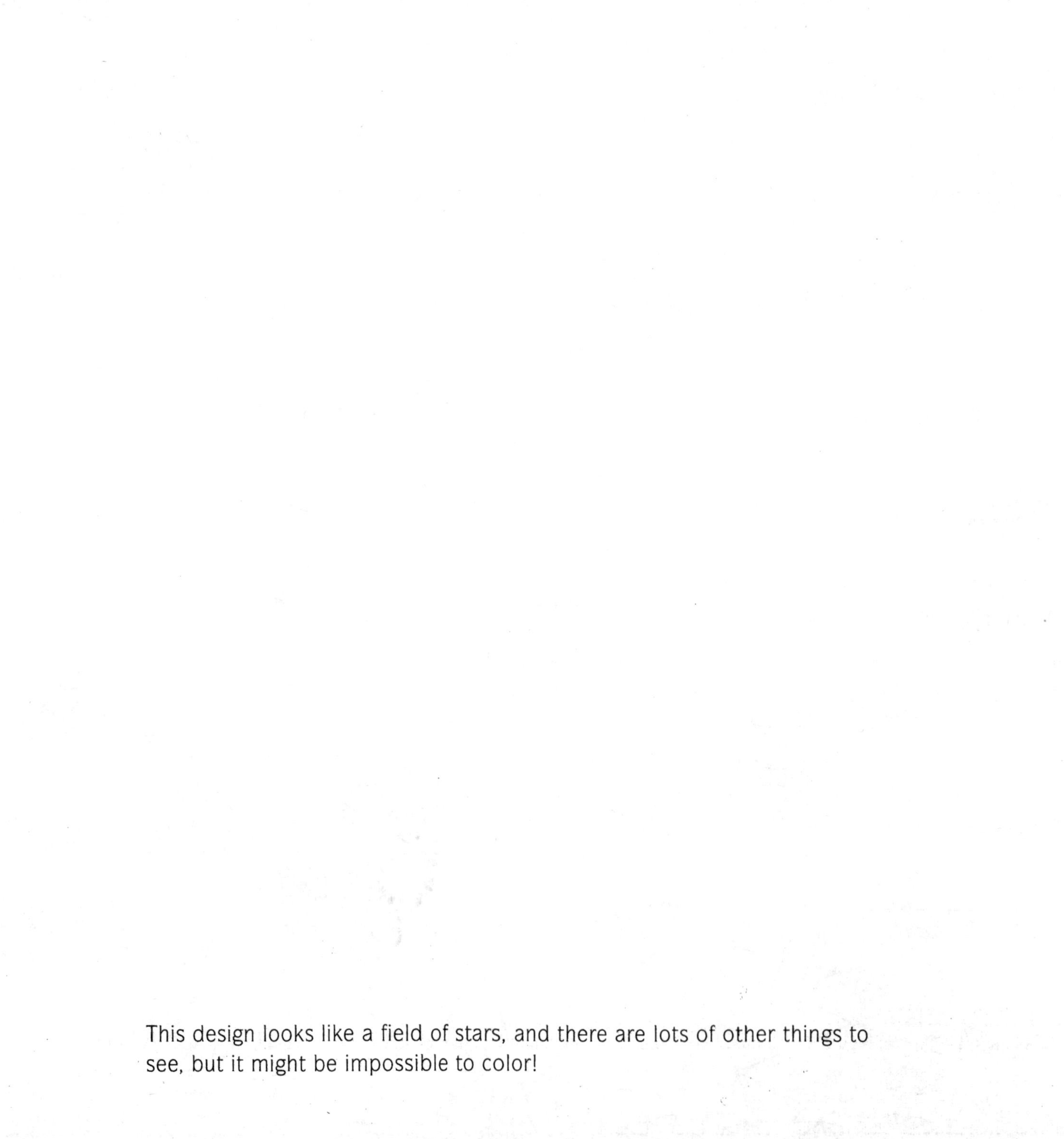

This design looks like a field of stars, and there are lots of other things to see, but it might be impossible to color!

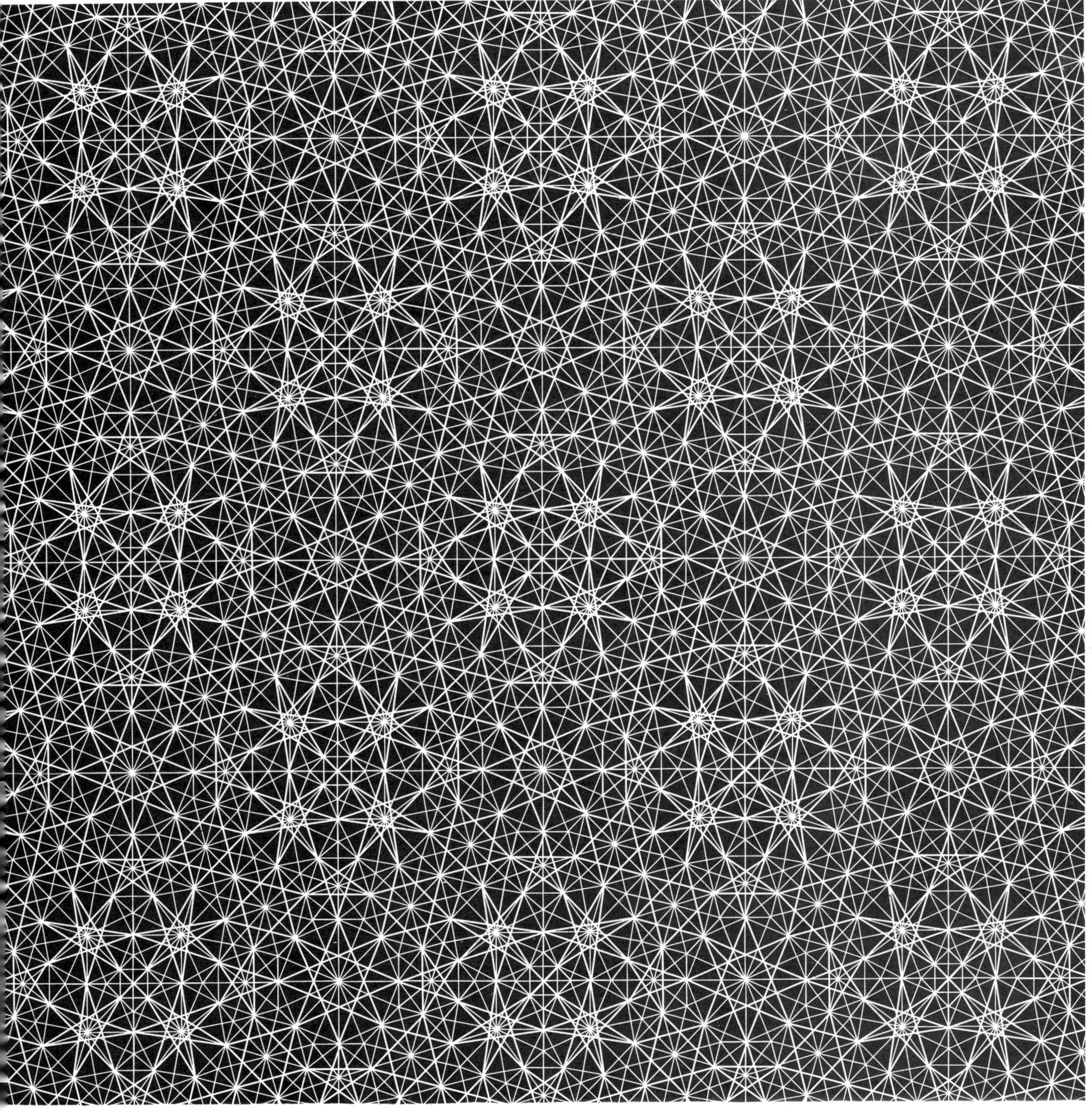

Roger Burrows is the author of about thirty books and papers on geometry, design, and architectural form. He is also a children's author and an inventor.

Check out Roger on www.sandviks.com and you'll see just a few of the unique children's products and technologies that he has created.

If you want to find out more about the mathematics of close-packing spheres and the other geometrical systems used to create *Images 5*, as well possible applications in architecture and physics, please write to Roger care of Running Press.